50 Recipes 25 Urban Talents 5 Cities

King Adz

Thames & Hudson

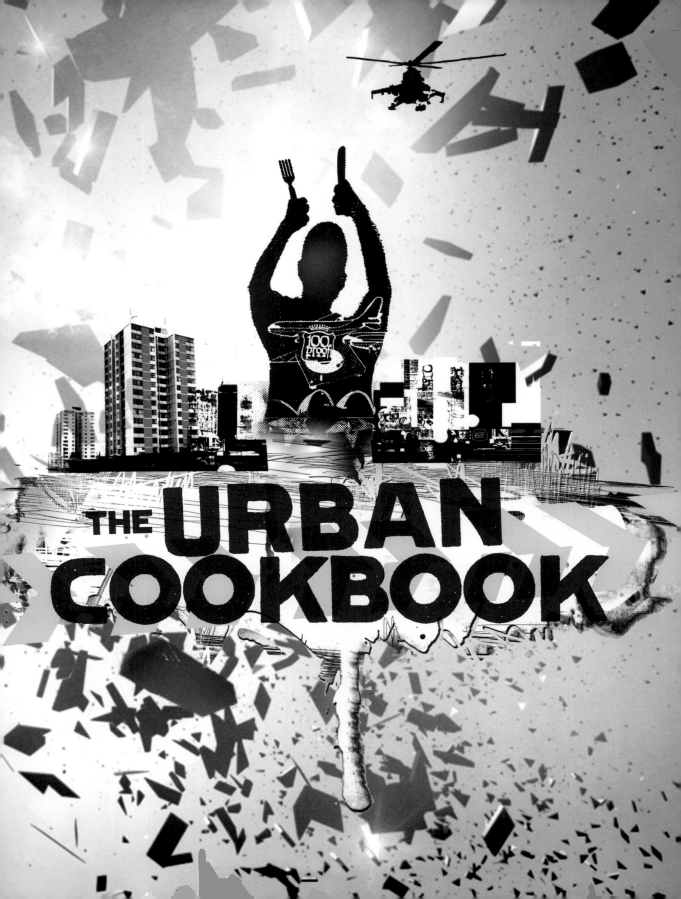

THE URBAN COOKBOOK

CONTENTS

6 Introduction

NEW YORK

PARIS

First published in the United Kingdom in 2008 by Thames & Hudson Ltd, 181A High Holborn, London WC1V 7QX

www.thamesandhudson.com

A dedicated website has been established to accompany this book:

www.urbancookbook.tv

© 2008 King Adz

British Library Cataloguing-in-Publication Data
A catalogue record for this book is available from the British Library

ISBN 978-0-500-51430-6

Printed and bound in Singapore by Craft Print International Ltd

Introduction

This is for everyone. Urban cookery (street food) is the most accessible form of cooking there is. Just as street art has brought the beauty of art into the lives of the masses, street food is all about making diverse and tasty food available to all, using simple recipes that are quick and easy to follow. There is no mystery, no special secret. Just turn the pages, check out the talents, follow the recipes and soon you'll have opened up a whole new world of food and culture.

Street food is anything that is cooked on BBQs, grills or braais, in cafés, diners, snack bars, chippies, takeaways, booths, cabins and food vans, and it has to be good, ethnically diverse and fresh, not 'fast' or 'junk'.

The one constant in my life and travels over the last twenty years has been my love of this street food. OK, so I've gone through a few career changes (from art director and animation director to film maker, culture vulture and travel and food writer), and I've lived and worked in four different continents (Europe, Africa, North America and Asia) but I've always been dedicated to the search for something new to eat on whatever street I happen to be schlepping along. It's like this: I spot an opening, a window of opportunity, and I'm like – surprise me! So I rock up, study the menu and order something I've never eaten before. If the food is good I spend the rest of the day working out how to cook it at home so I can recreate the taste that I experienced on the street. This usually takes a couple of attempts (and this is worth remembering), as it's all a matter of taste. Once I think I've cracked it, then I invite my crew around and make a meal of it!

Creativity in the street is all about expanding skills and knowledge and expressing ideas through urban culture. And food unites people the world over: we all have to eat, no matter what rules we live, work and play by. Travel is the only way to truly broaden your outlook. And urban life is all about the culture and the shared experiences of city people all over the world. So in many ways, this book is about getting together to break bread and share stories and talents. *The Urban Cookbook* therefore unites three concepts: creativity through urban culture, cooking and travel.

Most of the recipes in this book are from my most recent road trip, but some of them I've collected and developed over many years. They're not just cooking recipes, though: some of them are creative recipes, explaining how to make street art, sign a record deal or create original fashions. You can check out all of these recipes and ideas at www.urbancookbook.tv. So get your friends together, cook a meal from this book and talk all night long about urban creativity.

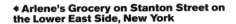

◆ Arlene's Grocery on Stanton Street on the Lower East Side, New York

King Adz **My creative journey**

Back inna day, I was going to be a chef, and although as a kid I loved advertising and mail order catalogues, and was always 'designing' cars and writing stories, I enjoyed cooking most of all (and spent hours experimenting in my suburban kitchen, away with the pixies).

I never got on very well at school and so as a fifteen-year-old I signed up to become an apprentice at a much hyped restaurant that my old man was involved with. But the restaurant opening was delayed for a couple of years and so I went to art school instead. I ended up at Central Saint Martins studying graphics (advertising) but was expelled in the final year and went to work for Bone Idol – a skate- and surf-wear company.

Around this time I started a creative collective called 100proof and set about developing the print advertising for Bone Idol. One thing led to another and soon I found myself working in South Africa as the art director of the DDB advertising agency. One of the directors there (Paul Sellars) worked with me on the creative for a soft drink aimed at women, and in the process he changed my career forever: his faith in my work encouraged me to

design print ads featuring European-style street art. When I found that there was nobody capable of producing the finished art work or TV spots in South Africa, I knocked out the images myself and ended up creating and directing the TV ads too.

But in the end, my ideas didn't appeal to the conservative Afrikaner clients: DDB lost the account, the creative was 'shelved' (read 'binned') and I was gutted. But on the bright side, I now had some experience and was able to convince a mate (John Pace), who was creative director of another ad agency, to let me direct something for Smirnoff. Which led to TV spot number two. And I then found another job in an ad agency in New York.

I had developed a taste for directing, however, so I moved back to England to work as a full-time director. Since then I've made music videos, commercials, indents, film titles, interstitials, short films, animated children's TV shows and documentaries. I still work in advertising from time to time, and if a brand needs an 'edgy', 'street' or 'urban' feel, then I'm your man. You do get pigeonholed and typecast. So my advice is to find yourself a niche and eventually, hopefully, the work will come your way.

➧ **Tagged burger boy at Astroland in Coney Island, Brooklyn**

King Adz **Urban Creativity**

How can you inspire creativity? How do you even define what it is? A tune, a painting, a sound, a view, a tag, a stencil, a dish, a move, a face, a look, a thought or a feeling…Everything and anything can inspire your creativity.

You need to walk the streets with your eyes open, love your fellow (wo)man and take time to hang with your nearest and dearest. Share your talents and spread the words (whatever they are).

I carefully researched and selected the talents featured in this book and sent them a short list of questions. Inspired by their answers (though they didn't all answer everything), I visited each one to check out their life, work and attitude to all things urban. Here are the questions I sent out before I got to know any of the talents involved. And just so you know where I'm coming from, I'm going to answer them myself first…

When were your formative years?
From 1985 to 1995.

Nearest city while growing up?
London.

Who, or what, has had an urban influence in the following areas?
MUSIC: *Men at Work, The Beat, DJ Shadow, DJ Cam, Lupe Fiasco and Lee 'Scratch' Perry.*
ART: *Andy Warhol, Keith Haring and Banksy.*
DESIGN: *Nathan Reddy, Saul Bass, Neville Garrick and Garth Walker.*
ADVERTISING/MEDIA: *Tony Kaye and Malcolm McLaren.*

▶ **'To be Sure of the Flavour' artwork for an advertising campaign proposal by King Adz**

FASHION: *Vivienne Westwood, Shawn Stüssy, Adidas and Skateware.*
FILM: *Krzysztof Kieslowski, Werner Herzog, Lars von Trier and Hype Williams.*
LITERATURE: *Martin Amis, Hunter S. Thompson and Tama Janowitz.*
CITY/PLACE: *London, Johannesburg and New York.*

How have you made your mark on urban culture?
I make films and books and PDFs about creativity, and try to inspire others to live in peace with fellow humans.

What made you realize that urban culture was changing?
When I went to a street art show and paintings were selling for £16,000. And when Banksy was first mentioned on CNN.

When was that?
In 2007.

Who should be recognized in this project?
All the shorties coming up in the world, flexing their street art and creative muscles for the first time, trying to earn a little respect, trying to flip it to another level; all those who try to create something new, when all they hear is: 'Everything's been done before.' Peeps like Wilma $, Dr. D and The Killer Gerbil.

What is your favourite food?
Indian/Pakistan (especially masala dosa), Cape Malay and braaivleis (South African BBQ).

"For the last twenty minutes of my flight to New York, a video loop plays on the small monitor in front of me, bombarding me with imagery of all things bling: diamonds, plasma screen TVs, surround sound systems, cars, luxury cruises, plastic surgery. I wonder if I'm missing something. Is this an orientation film for the American way of life? The message behind the film seems to be 'Welcome to the land of the free market.' But then I remember that in this land of opportunity and excess lies the small enclave of the Lower East Side."

NewYorkCity

is the Mecca of urban culture. I flew to Newark – the best way to get into NYC – and after I'd cleared immigration (fingerprints and mugshot) I got on the NJ Transit train to NY Penn Station. Instantly I spotted some fat wild style graffiti, and I got buzzed. It felt like I was home. The train rounded a corner and then I spotted the Manhattan skyline. I was hyped!

Some background info

Hip hop culture was born in the Bronx at the beginning of the 1970s when Kool Herc, a local DJ, invented break music, or B-beat, by playing two copies of the same instrumental break of funk and soul tunes back to back. The Incredible Bongo Band's 'Apache' became the national anthem of the Bronx for many years after it was released in 1973. Soon a friend of Kool DJ Herc began to shout lines over the break. And rap was born. Then Afrika Bambaataa began DJing with a similar B-beat style and took break music to the next level with his trademark phrases 'Shockin' on', 'Don't stop that bodyrock', 'Sureshot the bodyrock' and 'Coolin' out turn the place out'. Then Grandmaster Flash stepped up with longer, more sophisticated rhymes added over the B-beat music. The four cornerstones of hip hop culture came from this scene: DJing, rapping, break-dancing and graffiti.

◆ Katz's Delicatessen on the corner of East Houston and Ludlow Street on the Lower East Side, New York

Bowery / Lower East Side / First Park

Welcome to the Lower East Side – the only 'real' part of Manhattan left. The East Village (above the Lower East Side) has been taken over by the rich and trendy, forcing the remaining real people down into the 'Belly of the Beast' and out into Williamsburg, Brooklyn. To experience the real Lower East Side you have to get down with the Bowery bums. They are the Kings and Queens of the streets.

On arrival I find an ultra-swanky hotel smack bang in the middle of Bowery. The closure of the legendary music club CBGB heralded a change for the Lower East Side: the place was officially under gentrification.

The Lower East Side is truly representative of America – the rich hang with the artists and bohos, the down-and-outs play sax and drink from paper bags, and nobody cares. I started each day people-watching while drinking coffee in a small café on Houston and Avenue A. First of all I watched a taxi driver shunting cars as he squeezed his cab into a parking place that was way too small. The cars in front of and behind rocked and inched forward, but the sun was shining and everything was cool.

Coney Island

Coney Island is a seaside resort like no other. A once respectable beach that fell off the radar in the 1970s (when it was filled with used needles), it is now New York's very own 'Ghetto-on-Sea'. Nothing could have prepared me for what was to come when I took the F train from 2nd Avenue station: mental graff all the way from Brooklyn to the end of the line.

SEARCH&DESTROY
1977
30 FUCK'IN YEARS OF
PUNK
EXTRA
POWER
$$
WAKING UP
THE DEAD
SALE!

The Afro-American and Latino inhabitants of Brooklyn flood into Coney Island on summer weekends, carrying sound systems, bling, snakes and parrots into the tatty funfair and onto the patched-up boardwalk and the sandy beach. The place is rammed with hip hop influences and everyone rocks their freshest sneakers and street wear. And no trip is complete without a visit to Nathan's Famous hotdogs. Pile on the onions and coleslaw and try not to get it down your front on the way back to Manhattan.

Coney Island is a must in the summer, but there are rumours that a certain entertainment company wants to turn it into a proper resort, and so its days may be numbered.

Lower East Side/East Village walk

This is a great circular route of the Lower East Side and the East Village with an abundance of poster, sticker and stencil art on display everywhere. You can join at any point but I prefer to start and finish at Bowery. So, walk the walk. All you need to do is walk along Bowery until you reach East 4th Street. Take a right turn and keep walking until you reach the junction with 2nd Avenue, at which point, turn left and walk up to East 9th Street. Turn right onto this street and keep going, over 1st Avenue, until you reach the edge of Tompkins Square Park. Turn right onto Avenue A and walk alongside the park. Keep going right down to East Houston Street, where you should turn right, cross over the road and keep heading south along Ludlow Street. Once on Ludlow Street keep a look out for Stanton Street and turn right onto it at the first opportunity. Follow this street straight on for a few blocks, through the park, until you hit Bowery again. Finito.

It will take you the best part of a day if you leisurely check out these parks, shops, bars and eateries. Tompkins Square Park is definitely worth a wander – it's full of skaters, local freak-a-zoids and assorted street dwellers. Even the well heeled walk their dogs in the 'little' and 'big' dog runs there. And don't miss Katz's Deli on East Houston and Ludlow (see the Hit List): it's a traditional Manhattan deli and has to be experienced to be believed. Be prepared to use your elbows.

Once a hang out for New York punks like the New York Dolls, St Mark's Place has a real greasy vibe to it, even though it's being smartened up a bit. Search & Destroy (see Hit List) is the best place to shop for vintage and original punk clothes. Scene Kids would go ape-shit in here.

In the heart of the Lower East Side you will find the Max Fish bar on Ludlow Street (see the Hit List). This is my favourite place to hang – it's filled with skaters, graffiti legends, artists, rockers and punks. It has art on the walls and some well retro video games and pinball machines. And just round the corner in Stanton Street is Arlene's Grocery, a unique combination of grocery store and bar. I didn't do any shopping there, but the many interesting people hanging out in the bar after dark led me to believe it's a popular choice with the locals. The Mars Bar (see the Hit List) is another place worth checking out if you want to see the real Lower East Side at night. All the surfaces are scratched to fuck with graffiti, tags and drawings, and the punters are tattooed and pierced up.

The Sunday market in Orchard Street is good for vintage and secondhand clothes, as well as antiques and other bric-a-brac, while Patricia Field's clothes shop on Bowery has the campest shop assistants and the best gay- and punk-influenced fashion.

But the Lower East Side is a-changing. They've stuck a big glass hotel in the middle of it. You need to get there before it's completely gentrified and the magic is gone. Plan your own route, and check out everything that's going on around you. But most of all seek out the Bowery bums and listen to their stories. These are the real historians. Buy one a beer and they'll give you a guided tour of all their spots, if they can walk.

◆ **Search & Destroy on St Mark's Place in the East Village, New York**

Hit List

Indie shops

aNYthing
51 Hester Street

Frank's Chop Shop
19 Essex Street

Alife Rivington Club
158 Rivington Street

Reed Space
151 Orchard Street

Search & Destroy
25 St Mark's Place

Trash & Vaudeville
4 St Mark's Place

Shut Skates
158 Orchard Street

St. Mark's Comics
11 St Mark's Place

Food

Madras Café
79 2nd Avenue
(the best veggie curry in New York)

Katz's Delicatessen
205 East Houston Street
(old-school Jewish deli)

Royale
157 Avenue C
(great burgers)

Shake Shack
southeast corner of Madison Square Park,
near Madison Avenue and East 23rd Street
(the best burgers in New York)

Corner Bistro
331 West 4th Street
(more great burgers)

Cafés

Mud Coffee
307 East 9th Street
(the best hot beverages in New York)

Caffe Reggio
119 MacDougal Street
(a classic Italian café)

Bars

Mars Bar
25 East 1st Street

Max Fish
178 Ludlow Street

My iPod Playlist

Beastie Boys
Paul's Boutique

Nas
Illmatic

Lupe Fiasco
Food & Liquor

Moby
Remixes

Joy Division
'Transmission'

Colin Hay
acoustic version of 'Overkill'

Erick Sermon featuring Marvin Gaye
'Music'

The Clash
'Bank Robber'

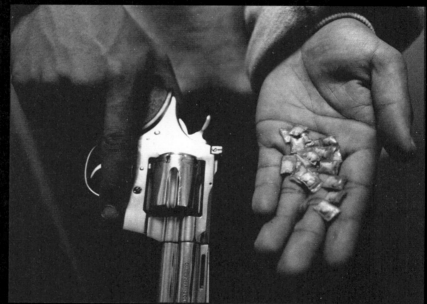

Boogie

Boogie was born in Serbia and emigrated to the United States in 1998. He is a photographer with an interest in all things urban, and has documented the New York gang scene, Cuba, Brazil, Gypsies, skinheads, crack and dope users and Hasidism. Through it all he has lived and worked in Brooklyn. His work has appeared in the *New York Times*, *Rolling Stone Magazine*, *TIME Magazine*, *Maxim* and *Playboy*, among many other publications, and his clients include Nike, Lee jeans, Element skateboards and Shellac.

www.artcoup.com

King Adz vs Boogie

When were your formative years?
From 1993 onwards.

Nearest city while growing up?
Belgrade, Serbia.

Who, or what, has had an urban influence in the following areas?
MUSIC: *The Cockney Rejects, Run-DMC and The White Stripes.*
ART: *No idea.*
DESIGN: *Morning Breath Inc.*
ADVERTISING/MEDIA: *Maximum Rock'n'Roll.*
FASHION: *Fred Perry and Ben Sherman.*
FILM: *Alan Clarke, Jim Jarmusch and Emir Kusturica.*
LITERATURE: *No idea.*
CITY/PLACE: *Brooklyn, New York.*

How have you made your mark on urban culture?
I just took a few photos.

What made you realize that urban culture was changing?
Culture always changes.

Who should be recognized in this project?
Kostas Seremetis.

What is your favourite food?
Stuffed dried peppers – a Serbian dish.

Photographs by Boogie ☞ ***Cut Meat**, 1997*
◄ ***Crack + Guns**, 2007* ☜ ***Payback**, 2007*
◄► ***True Love**, 2005*

BOOGIE
25

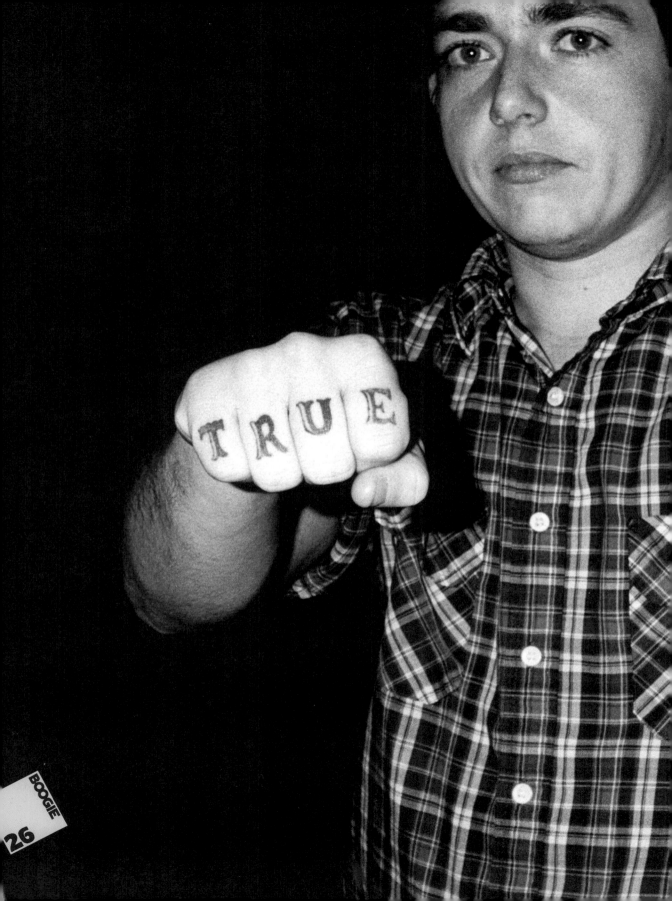

BOOGIE
27

Tristan Eaton

In the world of urban vinyl toys, Tristan is the big
dog. He designed his first toy for Fisher-Price
aged eighteen and has since worked with many
brands including Hasbro, Pepsi and Nike on
creative projects that have taken him from city
streets to gallery walls, and everywhere in between.

Tristan went on to create the legendary Dunny and
Munny toys for limited edition toy manufacturer
Kidrobot in 2003. These two toys defined the
designer vinyl toy genre as we know it today: just
check eBay and you'll find customized editions of
Tristan's toys by artists such as Shepard Fairey,
Dr Revolt, Quik, Dalek, Gary Baseman, Buff
Monster, David Flores, Ron English, Flying Fortress,
Queen Andrea and Sket One. New York's Museum
of Modern Art (MoMA) have included Dunny and
Munny in their permanent design collection.

He now runs the Thunderdog Collective – a
design studio and toy production company – in
the DUMBO (Down Under the Manhattan Bridge
Overpass) neighbourhood of Brooklyn, which
creates and markets the most progressive toys
in today's (rapidly expanding) market.

www.thunderdogstudios.com

King Adz vs *Tristan Eaton*

When were your formative years?
From 1985 to 1993.

Nearest city while growing up?
Los Angeles, London, Detroit and New York.

Who, or what, has had an urban influence in the following areas?
MUSIC: *Public Enemy.*
ART: *Mode 2.*
DESIGN: *The Designers Republic.*
ADVERTISING/MEDIA: *Shepard Fairey.*
FASHION: *Run-DMC.*
FILM: *Spike Lee is the obvious answer...Do The Right Thing.*
LITERATURE: *Zephyr.*
CITY/PLACE: *Brooklyn, New York.*

How have you made your mark on urban culture?
I helped start the urban vinyl toy industry in America. And I bombed a few walls on the way up.

What made you realize that urban culture was changing?
When Hasbro called me. And when Kidrobot went super-commercial.

When was that?
Three years ago.

Who should be recognized in this project?
Sket One (www.sket-one.com): the hardest working man in the toy biz. And he still pieces every Sunday!

What is your favourite food?
My mum's shepherd's pie, and her sausage rolls too.

TRISTAN EATON
30

TRISTAN
EATON

31

How to create genius toys
by Tristan Eaton

First you need a genius idea – which is hard to come by, as there seem to be a lot of crappy toys out there. People do make toys without a genius idea but it's helpful if you have one.

Once you have the inspiration, you have to figure how to articulate its functionality. There is a lot of conceptualizing at the beginning, before you start to draw. But once you have a good idea about what to do, you should take an analogue approach and draw it by hand. Draw it in six perspectives: from the front, back, left, right, top and bottom.

After hand-sketching the toy I usually scan the drawings and build up the artwork using 3D modelling – there are lots of different digital methods for doing it and I'm a real fan of all that.

When you have the idea drawn up to a good standard, send it off to the factory for the first wax sculpt (I use Chinese and American sculptors). This is probably the most exciting thing to see – it normally looks like shit the first time, but you can actually see your creation in front of you. You make some edits, draw on photographs of the wax, and work it until it's perfect. Sometimes this takes ten rounds of sending it back and forth to the sculptors.

When the toy is perfect, you sign it off and the factory will make a resin model, which shows you how the legs and arms will move, and you can make sure everything is going to work properly. Around this time you need to design packaging and send it off to the factory.

The factory then makes the master moulds and a decision has to be made about what kind of process to use – rotary-casting vinyl or injection-moulded vinyl? Rotary casting is cheap (it's a hollow figure) whereas injection-moulding gives you a solid piece of vinyl, which is more expensive. Sometimes you need a combination of both.

The moulds are then made and the first vinyl sample produced, which is totally unpainted, but you can see and feel how the toy is going to turn out. The paint designs are created from this sample and sent to the factory as Illustrator files for the graphics, pad printing and spray masking. Some are detailed patterns that wrap around the 3D forms. This is a really exciting part of the process. When the first graphics and paint samples come back they can be screwed up, but you have to see them working to be able to make them perfect.

Once this is done the toy goes into final production. Then you have all the fun and adventures of getting them sold!

CRAZY SUPERS

TOOLS

PARKS

THINGS I ♥ ABOUT NEW YORK

THE EVERYTHING BAGEL FROM LA BAGEL DELIGHT

SNOW FALLING OVER THE CITY

SUBWAY RUNS 24/7

BAR

F

DOG FRIENDLY BARS

Jon Setzen

Jon is a graphic artist who has travelled the world to find inspiration for his unique urban fantasy. Using Photoshop to manipulate his own photos, Jon's creations combine futurist and retro images with pictures of nature and wildlife: animals roam the city, boats fly and planes swim, while giraffes stroll the streets and cable cars swing between tower blocks, all under a graphic rainbow.

www.standardmotion.com

King Adz vs Jon Setzen

When were your formative years?
From the age of thirteen onwards.

Nearest city while growing up?
San Francisco.

Who, or what, has had an urban influence in the following areas?
MUSIC: *The Velvet Underground, Charlie Parker, The Smiths and Hefner.*
ART: *Weegee, Gerhard Richter, Todd Hido and Jean-Michel Basquiat.*
DESIGN: *Saul Bass, Reid Miles, Peter Saville, Robert Brownjohn and Rick Griffin.*
ADVERTISING/MEDIA*: Ray Gun magazine, Drawn and Quarterly magazine and Nike ads.*
FASHION: *LRG Clothing, Modern Amusement Clothing and Adidas.*
FILM: *Woody Allen, Jean-Pierre Jeunet and David Simon.*
LITERATURE: *James Baldwin, Caleb Carr and Irvine Welsh.*
CITY/PLACE: *New York.*

How have you made your mark on urban culture?
I feel that all of us who live within the definition of an urban environment contribute to urban culture. I started making show posters at a time when there was a lack of good original posters for shows in New York. Most of them were generic flimsy mailer labels. So when I was approached by Mikey Palms and Matt Roff to bring back the idea of promoting a special musical

event at their new venue, I agreed. It didn't take long before other artists and designers started making posters again and there has definitely been an increase in the amount of hand-made posters up at venues around New York. I like to think, if anything, that I encouraged people to put pen to paper (so to speak) and get involved with promoting good music, smaller bands and venues that are not controlled by corporations.

What made you realize that urban culture was changing?
Culture has always been changing. New York benefits from the large number of people coming into the city everyday. I tried to set up a design collective in San Francisco, but everyone was too consumed with their ridiculously well-paid yet meaningless dot.com jobs. I include myself in that category. But after moving to New York I couldn't go back to the nine-to-five lifestyle and needed to live life without

an alarm clock. There's a hunger in New York to work hard, collaborate and actually accomplish things. Maybe it's because there's a fear that there are so many people doing what you do that if you turn down a project, someone else will pick it up. The end of the dot.com era got creative people out of their cushy offices and back onto the street, where they were forced to forget about templates and sponsorship. They needed to concentrate on finding a voice and starting over instead. I know more freelancers nowadays than I ever did before. No one wants to work in an office. Every time I go out I meet people to create work with or for. It's inspiring and fulfilling.

Who should be recognized in this project?
I would recommend nature. The idea of the 'urban' seems to centre too much around concrete, subways and masses of people. Obviously they are the backbone and definition of what 'urban' really is, but in any urban environment, nature still exists. The lack of nature in an urban area makes nature even more celebrated within the city: what would New York be without Central Park, or Brooklyn without Prospect Park? The juxtaposition of nature and urbanity is one of the more beautiful things about being in a city. To find a small patch of grass or a massive tree amongst towering buildings is calming and something I could never live without.

What is your favourite food?
Tacos carne asada (beef tacos) from La Taqueria in San Francisco.

Rodney Smith

Rodney is one of the founding fathers of the East Coast skate scene, and it was because of his love of wheels and motion that he first got hold of his older brother's discarded board and began to skate in 1978. Rodney has never looked back. He was even one of the first East Coast street skaters to be sponsored (by Variflex in 1983).

The New York skate scene played a massive part in the formation of street skating as a worldwide phenomenon. Rodney started the Shut crew – the first ever New York City-based skateboard company – in 1986. Shut is one of the few skate teams, and skate companies, to operate like a family unit: it consists of a core group of skaters who have been a vital element of the New York City skate scene from the start.

Rodney ran the company successfully until 1992, when he and business partner Bruno Musso closed it down. Rodney then directed his attention towards keeping the Shut legacy alive under a new name. This was when Zoo York was conceived, with Eli Morgan Gesner and Adam Schatz. The Shut Skates team included Jefferson Pang, Sean Sheffey, Coco Santiago, Chris Pastras, Barker Barrett, Jeremy Henderson and Félix Argüelles, to name a few.

Through a love of skating and an appreciation of hip hop, art and the urban underground, Zoo York grew into a globally successful company. After taking on other partners, Rodney and company had a difference of opinion about the direction in which the brand should go. Rodney, Eli and Adam pulled Shut out of hibernation and it was business as before, getting back to their roots and the bare bones of creativity. Today, Shut has cultivated a massive network of family members, who are fiercely loyal and stand behind the brand one hundred per cent. Shut has created an amazing and authentic range of boards and skate apparel (see Rodney's creative recipe, p. 42).

www.shutnyc.com

King Adz vs *Rodney Smith*

When were your formative years?
In the late 1970s I was an elementary-age skateboarder and a BMX enthusiast; by the early 1980s I was a teenage city explorer and youth movement follower; from the mid-1980s to 2007 I was an East Coast/NYC skateboard industry co-pioneer.

Nearest city while growing up?
New Brunswick in New Jersey, a small city populated by Rutgers University students.

Who, or what, has had an urban influence in the following areas?
MUSIC: *KRS-One, Bad Brains, Murphy's Law and the Beastie Boys.*
ART: *Futura 2000, STASH and Crazy Legs.*
DESIGN: *Eli Morgan Gesner.*
ADVERTISING/MEDIA: *Nike (what if all athletes were treated this way?)*
FILM: *The Van Peebles.*
LITERATURE: *Ralph Ellison.*
CITY/PLACE: *New York, and specifically, CBGB.*

How have you made your mark on urban culture?
By being a mentor to young kids via skateboarding, and by being one of the founders of NYC's first skateboard manufacturing company, showing people that a skateboarding business can survive on the 'other' coast.

What made you realize that urban culture was changing?
I suppose it had to be when each and every bit of urban culture moved from its core beginnings and became mainstream. I recognized things like that way back, only I didn't know whether these cultures would suffer or prosper in the long term.

When was that?
It was around 1978.

Who should be recognized in this project?
Jeremy Henderson.

What is your favourite food?
Any home-cooked Asian food.

RODNEY SMITH

49

RODNEY
SMITH
41

How to create authentic skate products
by Rodney Smith

Living in a big city exposes me to all styles of fashion, and every shape, size and colour. I am influenced by what makes people feel comfortable and secure rather than current styles in fashion, although you do have to take some trends into consideration.

At Shut we try to look at popular youth trends and balance them with what we would wear ourselves. Then I speak to my partners Adam and Eli and we design mostly by democracy. We have to look at what will be popular because we want our products to work. Obviously we want to get it right, but we also try to cater to everyone's taste. Looking back at what worked previously is a great way to bring something of the past into the here and now: we are still into urban classics like 501 jeans, the hightop Adidas shell toe, Nike court force and red Russell sweatpants. But the market is wide open right now, and I can also take a different design approach because there is a resurgence of skateboard styles and shapes coming back into the picture.

I try to be original in my designs both shape-wise and graphically. But back-to-basics is the key to attracting contemporary customers to the Shut brand. If you go all out for edgy, or try to catch on to a trend a little too late, you will lose sales in the end. You have to be true to what you are about and where you have come from so that the product reflects authenticity and serves the customer well.

Wooster Collective

Marc and Sara Schiller began the Wooster Collective in 2001. At first it was a personal blog that commented on the ephemeral art that had begun to appear ever more frequently on streets all over the world. The site has now morphed into the ultimate resource and guide to all things street art related and has over 100,000 subscribers.

Street art may have been born from the New York graffiti scene in the 1980s, but it has followed its own path since then, with graffiti writers staying true to illegal graffiti, and street artists embracing the art scene for all it's worth, including exhibiting in galleries (see London, p. 213). Banksy, Obey, Swoon, D*Face, Brad Downey, Invader and Blek le Rat, are just a few of the artists who have pushed urban art forward to a whole new level. And it is this pioneering work that is documented by the Wooster Collective.

In 2006 Marc and Sara began work on the Wooster on Spring project at 11 Spring Street in Soho, New York. This had been a favourite address for street art over the years, but the building was to be renovated and turned into exclusive apartments. Marc and Sara cut an extraordinary deal with the developers and were allowed to turn the interior and exterior of the building into a monument to street and ephemeral art. Many of the world's most talented street artists visited to create their art, and the building was opened to the public for three days in December 2006, with queues of people waiting five hours to get in.

www.woostercollective.com

♦♦♦ The Wooster on Spring project in December 2006 at 11 Spring Street in Soho, New York

WOOSTER COLLECTIVE

45

King Adz vs *Wooster Collective*

When were your formative years?
During the late 1970s and early 1980s when I first saw films by John Cassavetes, Jean-Luc Godard, Wim Wenders, Francis Ford Coppola and Martin Scorsese **(Marc)**; *from 1990 to 1995 when I was running around the underground clubs in New York* **(Sara)**.

Nearest city while growing up?
Los Angeles **(Marc)**; *Bangor, Maine* **(Sara)**.

Who, or what, has had an urban influence in the following areas?
MUSIC: *The Clash, Lou Reed, The Rolling Stones and Patti Smith.*
ART/PHOTOGRAPHY: *Jenny Holzer, Terry Richardson, Larry Clark, Ryan McGinley, Barbara Kruger, Daido Moriyama, Andy Warhol, Banksy, Jean-Michel Basquiat and Keith Haring.*
DESIGN: *Tibor Kalman and Milton Glaser.*
ADVERTISING/MEDIA: *Paper Magazine, the 'Absolut ——' vodka ad campaign and CNN.*
FASHION: *Dr Martens, Vivienne Westwood, Patricia Field, Adidas and green camouflage from the US Army.*
FILM: *John Cassavetes, Spike Lee and Frederick Wiseman.*
LITERATURE: *John Fante, Charles Bukowski, Tama Janowitz and Jay McInerney.*
CITY/PLACE: *Brooklyn, the Bronx, Queens and Lower Manhattan.*

How have you made your mark on urban culture?
We launched the Wooster Collective website, and we also curate and produce the Wooster on Spring exhibitions.

What made you realize that urban culture was changing?
When we saw a few years ago that tens of thousands of people were visiting the Wooster Collective website each day, which they had found completely by word of mouth.

When was that?
2001.

Who should be recognized in this project?
Richard Hambleton, John Fekner, Lady Pink and Doze Green.

What is your favourite food?
Sushi and Cuban corn-on-the-cob.

RASJAD'S
PERFECT
STEAK
48

Rasjad's perfect steak

This is a wicked steak marinade recipe I have nicked from my uncle Rasjad in Cape Town, but it's included in the chapter on New York cos the Yanks love a great steak. Once they read this recipe they will surely adopt it as their own…. You really need a fillet (or half) of beef for this recipe. You can use sirloin or rump but it won't taste the same.

Feeds 2–4
1 kg/2¼lb (or half the amount) **beef fillet/tenderloin, cut into steaks**

Marinade
25ml/1fl oz **soy sauce**
4 teaspoons **garlic paste from a jar**
2 teaspoons **ginger paste from a jar**
2 teaspoons **Worcestershire sauce**
25ml/1fl oz **sesame oil**

- Combine all of the marinade ingredients in a large mixing bowl. Then add the steaks, mix well and just cover with water. Leave for a day or so in the fridge.
- Cook the steaks on a hot BBQ or grill until the way you like them, and serve with fresh rolls and salad.

RASJAD'S PERFECT STEAK 51

Penne in vodka sauce

This recipe is the tastiest pasta dish ever, and really easy to make too. Pretend you're in the New York mafia when you're eating it…

Feeds 4
salt and black pepper
a tablespoon **of butter**
3 **cloves garlic, chopped**
120g/4oz **assorted Italian meat**
  (Parma ham, salami etc.), **thinly sliced**
2 cans **chopped tomatoes**
1 teaspoon **sugar**
2 **red chillies, chopped**
25ml/1fl oz **vodka**
500g/18oz **penne pasta**
150ml/5fl oz **cream**
freshly grated Parmesan

- Put a large pan of salted water on to boil.

- Melt the butter in a large frying pan, add the garlic and fry for a couple of minutes. Then add the sliced meat and fry for a further 5 minutes. Add the tomatoes, sugar, chilli and some black pepper, and cook for 5 minutes before adding the vodka.

- Then it's time to put the pasta into the boiling water and cook for 10 minutes (or whatever it says on the packet).

- When the pasta is ready, add the cream to the tomato sauce and cook gently for 2 minutes. While this is simmering, drain the pasta and put back into the big pan.

- Add the tomato sauce to the pasta and mix well.

- Cover with grated Parmesan and serve.

I ♥
PASTA

I GOT
ITALI
Attit

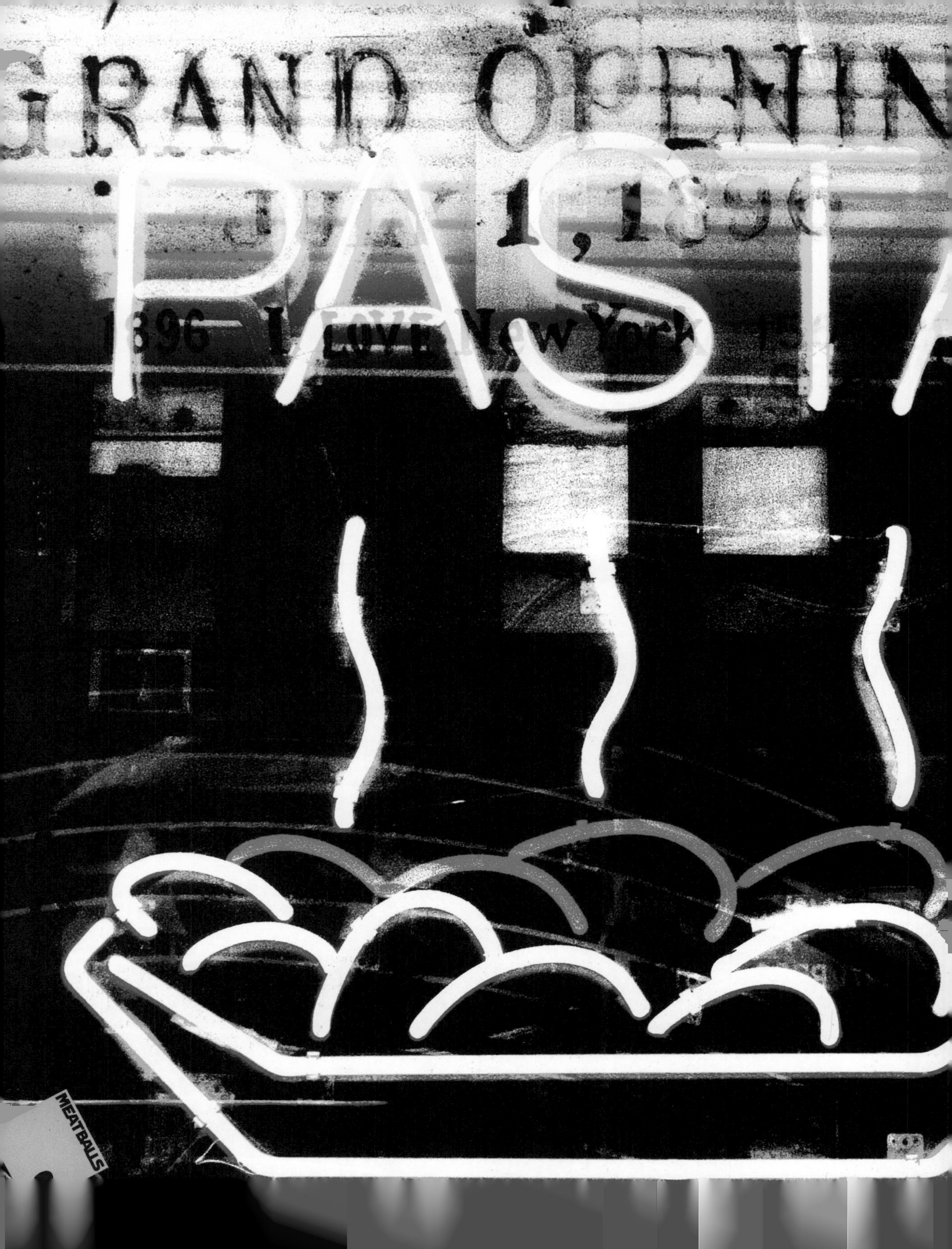
GRAND OPENIN
1896 I LOVE New York
MEATBALLS

Meatballs and spaghetti

More big props to Little Italy and all Italian-Americans. This is the sort of dish you get in any authentic Italian neighbourhood restaurant in New York.

Feeds 4

Meatballs

500g/1lb 2oz **minced ground beef or steak**
100g/¾ cup **matzo meal**
20g/¼ cup **Parmesan, grated**
1 **egg**
2 **teaspoons dried basil**
2 **teaspoons dried oregano**
1 **medium onion, finely chopped**
3 **cloves garlic, chopped**
salt and black pepper
a splash **of red wine**
125ml/4fl oz/½ cup **milk**

Tomato sauce

2 tablespoons **olive oil**
3 **cloves garlic, chopped**
1 large can **chopped tomatoes**
3 teaspoons **tomato purée**
2 teaspoons **dried basil**
1 teaspoon **sugar**
a pinch **of salt**

450g/1lb **of your favourite pasta variety**

- For the meatballs, mix all the ingredients together except for the milk. Then add a little of the milk at a time until the mixture is moist and the meat sticks together (not too moist). Shape small amounts of meat into palm-sized balls and place on a lightly greased baking tray.

- Bake in the oven at 200°C/400°F/Gas 6 for 30 minutes, until they are evenly browned.

- For the sauce, heat the oil in a large pan over a medium heat. Add the garlic and cook for 3 minutes. Stir in the remaining ingredients. Bring to the boil and then reduce the heat so that the sauce simmers uncovered for about 10 minutes.

- When the meatballs are nearly cooked, start boiling the pasta. Remove the meatballs from the oven and place gently into the tomato sauce. Drain the pasta and serve with the meatballs and sauce.

MEATBALLS

55

Beef in black bean sauce

Some of the best Chinese food I've ever eaten is to be found in New York's Chinatown. I like this dish best when served on a hot day in busy NYC. This recipe can also be used with chicken (wings are good), fish or prawns.

Feeds 4–6

700g/1lb 9oz **good-quality steak (rump, sirloin or fillet)**

1 tablespoon **soy sauce**

2 teaspoons **each of ginger and garlic pastes from a jar**

1 tablespoon **chilli bean sauce (from a Chinese supermarket)**

a splash **of cooking sherry**

2 tablespoons **cooking oil**

300ml/½ pint/1¼ cups **chicken stock**

3 **spring onions, finely chopped**

1 tablespoon **black beans (from a Chinese supermarket)**

1 **onion, chopped into 8**

1 **red and 1 green (or yellow) peppers**

1 tablespoon **cornflour, mixed with** 1 tablespoon **water to a paste**

- Slice the beef finely across the grain of the meat at an angle.

- Mix together the soy sauce, 1 teaspoon each of the garlic and ginger paste, the chilli bean sauce and the sherry. Marinate the sliced meat in the mixture for as long as you can, the longer the better.

- Remove the meat from the marinade, lightly fry in the oil, and put to one side.

- Put the chicken stock in a frying pan with the spring onion, the remaining garlic and ginger pastes and the black beans. Bring to the boil and simmer for about 3 minutes. Add the onion segments plus the peppers (chopped small or large as desired). Thicken with the cornflour paste.

- Add the fried beef, and cook together for a few minutes. Serve with boiled rice.

Three-egg omelette

This is very quick to make, and very tasty.
As available in any good café in the East Village…

Feeds 1
2 tablespoons **butter**
2 **cloves garlic, chopped**
2 **tomatoes, quartered**
8 **mushrooms, chopped**
1 handful **spinach leaves**
black pepper
3 **eggs, beaten**
115g/4oz **Cheddar cheese, grated**

- Melt half the butter in a small pan and fry the garlic gently. Add the tomatoes, mushrooms, spinach and some black pepper and cook for 5 minutes.

- In a separate frying pan, melt the remaining butter and when hot, pour in the egg mixture.

- Fry for 3 minutes, making sure the egg does not stick to the pan by slipping a spatula around the edges. Add the vegetables from the other pan into the middle of the omelette, and cover with grated cheese. Gently fold the omelette in half, and flip over.

- Serve with buttered toast, a cup of tea and a splash of brown sauce.

Meatloaf

Meatloaf is available in any American diner. I've bastardized this recipe a bit and added some healthier ingredients…

Feeds 4

500g/1lb 2oz **minced ground beef or steak**
1 **medium onion, finely chopped**
1 **beef stock cube**, dissolved in 225ml/8fl oz/1 cup boiling water
salt and black pepper
2 **carrots, grated**
100g/1½ cups **button mushrooms, chopped**
4 teaspoons **mixed herbs**
75g/½ cup **pine nuts**
a splash **of cooking sherry or red wine**
matzo meal
vegetable oil, for greasing

- In a large mixing bowl, mix together the mince, onion, stock, gravy browning, salt and pepper. Add the vegetables, herbs, nuts and a good splash of wine. The mixture should be fairly wet at this stage.

- Now add some matzo meal: start with 25g/1oz and add more, bit by bit, until the mixture is thickened but still quite moist.

- Grease a 900g/2lb loaf tin and then chuck in some matzo meal; shake it around the tin until it coats the greasy surface and tip out the excess. Put the mixture into the loaf tin and bake in the oven at 190°C/375°F/Gas 5 for about 1 hour. The meatloaf shrinks from the edges when cooked and should slip easily from the tin. When it is ready, tip it on to a plate or tray and give it another 5–10 minutes in the oven to brown.

- The meatloaf can be served hot or cold with salads or potatoes and vegetables. It also makes great sandwiches and leftovers can be chopped up and added to fried rice. What goes in it is a matter of taste, so experiment with the ingredients.

MEATLOAF
57

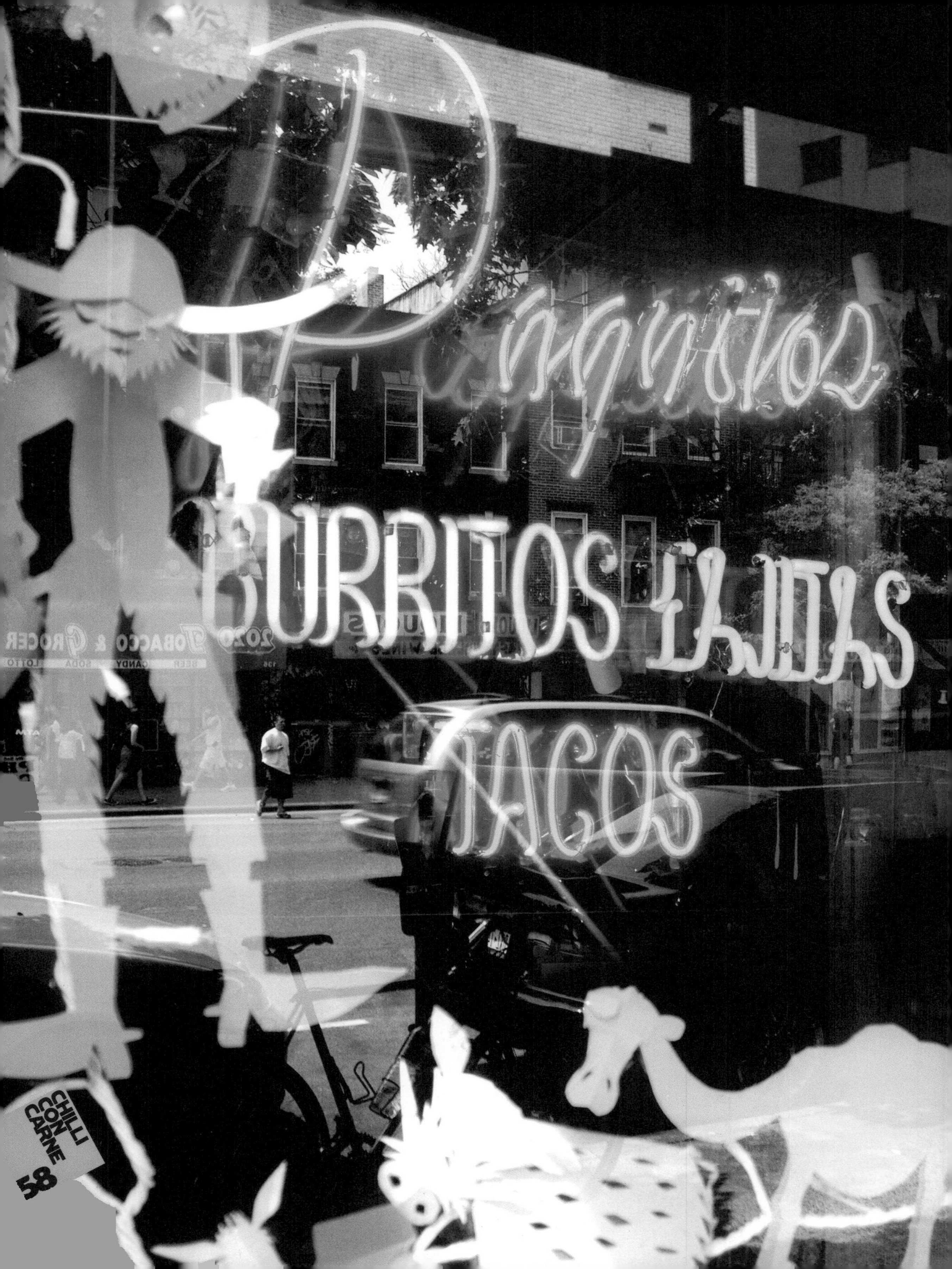
BURRITOS
TACOS

Chilli con carne

Coming up from the South! New York is where the best Tex-Mex is to be found. This chilli recipe is authentic and well healthy. And it tastes like it's straight from a street vendor or small café on the Lower East Side.

- Heat the vegetable oil in a large pan. Add the onion and fry gently for 5 minutes. Add the meat, allow to brown, and cook for a further 5 minutes.

- Then tip in the tomatoes, the tomato purée, lemon juice, the salt, red kidney beans, garlic, all the spices, the bay leaf and beef stock. Mix well and simmer for at least an hour, stirring occasionally (feel free to add more water if the mixture gets too thick). Cook for as long as possible.

- Stir the sour cream in at the last minute, and serve with tacos and baked potatoes on the side.

Feeds 4

3 tablespoons **vegetable oil**
1 large **onion, chopped**
500g/1lb 2oz **minced ground beef or steak**
2 cans **tomatoes**
1 tablespoon **tomato purée**
juice of ½ **lemon**
1 teaspoon **salt**
1 can **red kidney beans**
2 teaspoons **finely chopped garlic**
1 teaspoon **paprika**
1 teaspoon **cayenne pepper**
2 teaspoons **chilli powder**
2 teaspoons **fajita spice**
1 **bay leaf**
475ml/17fl oz/a generous 2 cups **beef stock**
3 tablespoons **sour cream**

Royal burger

The king of street food – the mighty burger! I had a few of these during my stay in New York. And be sure to check the Hit List (p. 20) for the best places to eat a burger there if you don't fancy cooking yourself.

Feeds 4
½ **onion, finely chopped**
1 **hard-boiled egg, shelled and chopped**
2 **teaspoons garlic paste from a jar**
500g/1lb 2oz **minced ground beef or steak**
2 teaspoons **mixed dried herbs**
a good dash **of BBQ sauce**
240ml/8fl oz/1 **cup beef stock**
matzo meal or breadcrumbs
grated cheese (optional)
peri-peri spice blend/chilli sauce

- In a large bowl, mix the chopped onion, egg, garlic and minced steak together well.

- Add the herbs, BBQ sauce and beef stock so that the mixture is pretty wet. Allow the whole thing to stand for 10 minutes before adding enough matzo meal or breadcrumbs to bind the mixture and make it less wet. The mixture should be quite moist but firm.

- Add the grated cheese (optional) and the peri-peri spice blend or chilli sauce to the bowl, mix well and form into burger patties. The patties can be any size you want. These burgers are best cooked on a BBQ until done to your taste. Serve with a toasted sesame seed bun and any of the following options: tons of peri-peri spice blend (this is how I have it), salad (lettuce, tomato and cucumber), and Caesar dressing.

"Paris has changed a lot over the past ten years: it is cleaner, and safer than ever before, but there are more police (les flics) and a more defined division of wealth. Most of the once abundant street art and graffiti is now gone, although there are a few spots left where you can find something really special."

Paris

Paris is a modern mix of many urban cultures – traditional French (the cafés, the bistros, the bars) alongside a large and mixed population of Algerians, Moroccans, Nigerians, Ivorians, Indians, French-Indians, African-French and Parisian-Moroccans. You can find the French standing in a bar drinking Ricard at eight in the morning, smoking fags like they're going out of style and talking about politics, but look around and there will be a crew of teetotal Muslim Arabs or Africans drinking strong coffee and talking in their own tongue. Eating couscous while you are in Paris is a must (see the Hit List, and the recipe on p. 100). It is a Berber dish in origin and is the main staple food throughout Algeria, eastern Morocco, Tunisia and Libya; it is also popular with the Jews of north Africa. In France, couscous is served with vegetables (carrots, swede and celery) and meat (beef, chicken or merguez, a north African sausage) and is cooked in a spicy broth.

Bastille

The rue de la Roquette (in the 11th arrondissement) runs east from the Place de la Bastille to the Place Léon Blum. It's at the heart of the nouveau rock movement in Paris and is full of bars and venues. The Parisians like their heroes a bit rough round the edges (Serge Gainsbourg, Johnny Halliday, Mickey Rourke) and the Bastille area is just the same: coarse but cool. I spent an afternoon in Café Divan (see Hit List) writing up my notes and checking out the young hipster locals.

La Chapelle

La Chapelle (in the 18th and 19th arrondissements) used to be La Crackhell, but the Indians and Sri Lankans moved in and sorted out the area. The smell of junk has been replaced by incense, and instead of the faces of jakeys trying to score on street corners, Bollywood stars beam out of movie posters on every shop and internet café window.

A few hundred metres to the west is Montmartre, which is tourist hell in the summer and always rammed with people looking for the Sacré Coeur at the top of the hill and Amélie's café (Le Verre à Pied, 118bis rue Mouffetard, in case you're interested). I checked into my hotel and then schlepped around looking for something decent to eat. I soon found Café Bharath, a great Sri Lankan restaurant (see the Hit List), which was full of Indians and Sri Lankans (always a good sign), and ended up eating as many wicked and authentic South Indian and Sri Lankan dishes as I could.

◆ A view of Paris from Sacré Coeur

Belleville

Belleville (in the 20th arrondissement) is Paris at its best: artistic, underground, laid back and raw. It's far from chic, but it's definitely for real. Arabs and Jews live side by side without any problems, and halal and kosher butchers sit next to each other on the street. To get there, take the (navy blue) Métro line 2 to Belleville.

A group of emerging street artists made Belleville their home at the beginning of the new millennium. Over the past five years I have documented the streets of this neighbourhood, especially the rue Dénoyez, which is home to one of the last remaining great walls of street art in Paris. Belleville's creative atmosphere and urban eclecticism helped to spawn l'École de Belleville, a loose, unintentional school of street artists, including l'Atlas, 'G', Invader (see p. 92) and JR (see p. 82).

Although all of them are street artists, some of them now sell their work in galleries around the world. During my time in Paris I hung out with 'G' and l'Atlas and watched them at work in their studios in La Forge – a chilled community of artists' studios smack bang in the middle of Belleville.

'G' creates massive urban *trompe l'oeils* from photos he has taken and blown up to the size of a billboard. He then adds colour and pastes his work up in the streets of Paris, strategically placing it at pavement level so as to create the optical illusion of a scene within a scene. Once the poster is up, 'G' takes a photo, usually with someone walking past reacting to the image, and the art is complete.

L'Atlas was busy making the first of his 3D pieces when I visited him, although he is mainly known for his distinctive typographic tagging. L'Atlas was due to participate in the annual Festival Kosmopolite in Bagnolet (an eastern suburb of Paris) so we checked it out together (see Hit List). The festival celebrates graffiti, hip hop, and all things urban. Each year the organizers bring over a different group of graffiti artists from around the world and Bagnolet is taken over by the specially erected billboards and the designated graffiti and street art walls, painted by guests and local artists alike.

French hip hop

The French are big into their hip hop. There are fly posters everywhere for national and international hip hop stars, and Generations FM 88.2 is a young, fresh Parisian radio station dedicated to hip hop acts like IAM, Fonky Family, Psy 4 De La Rime, 3ème Oeil, Boramy, Asso, B.O. digital and Kamelancien. Many French hip hop artists, including Lunatic, Mafia K1 Fry, La Brigade, Secteur Ä and Less Du Neuf, are from the banlieues, and this is often reflected in their lyrics denouncing the hardship of suburban life in Paris.

DJ Dee Nasty is the father of Parisian hip hop and was one of the first French DJs to promote hip hop, on his Radio Nova show. He first discovered hip hop in 1979 and began DJing in 1981. He is best known for producing the first French hip hop record, 'Panam City Rappin', in 1984, but he was also Disco Mix Club (DMC) Champion of France from 1986 to 1988 and European DMC Champion in 1990.

♦ A shop window in Montmartre displaying a kitch bust of Liberté

Hit List

Food

Aux Bons Amis
1, rue de l'Atlas (the best Belleville couscous in Paris)

Café Bharath
67, rue Louis Blanc
(the best Indian/Sri Lankan in Paris)

Café Divan
60, rue de la Roquette

Viet Siam
1, rue de l'Atlas (a great Belleville Vietnamese, next door to Aux Bons Amis)

Shopping

Colette
213, rue Saint-Honoré (gadgets, cosmetics, clothes and a bar too)

T-Maxx Records
111, rue Saint-Denis

Clubs/festivals

Club Élysée Montmartre
72, boulevard de Rochechouart

Festival Kosmopolite
www.kosmopolite.com

Street art resources

Website for l'Atlas
www.latlas.net

Website for 'G'
http://human.ist.free.fr

Sun 7 website
www.myspace.com/sun777

Une Nuit
street art book published by Kitchen 93 (www.kitchen93.com)

My iPod Playlist

Genius/GZA
Liquid Swords

DJ Cam
Substances (see p. 76)

Scientist
Scientist Wins the World Cup

Talking Heads
Remain in Light

David Sylvian
the instrumental side of the double album *Gone to Earth*

Mobb Deep
The Infamous

Brasse Vannie Kaap
BVK

Sigur Rós
Von

◆ **Invader's mosaics and a street dweller in the Belleville neighbourhood of Paris**

PARIS 69

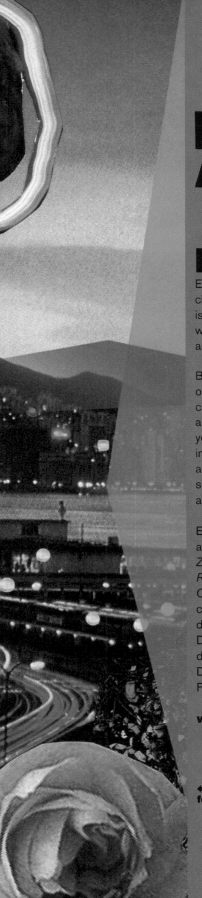

Elisabeth Arkhipoff

In this era of computer-generated and digitally manipulated imagery, artist and designer Elisabeth Arkhipoff bucks the trend and chooses instead to work with her hands. She is a graduate of Paris X University, and began working professionally in 2000. She now lives and works in Paris and New York.

Born in the Ivory Coast in 1973, Elisabeth is of Russian and Armenian descent: her mixed cultural heritage has helped her to collect a massive library of retro images over the years. She mixes these pictures with modern influences in order to create a unique style across many media, including music, painting, sculpture, photography, video, installation and drawing.

Elisabeth's work has featured in magazines and newspapers such as *Frieze*, *Süddeutsche Zeitung*, *Creative Review*, *IDEA*, *ZOO*, *Vogue*, *Ryuko Tsushin*, *+81*, *Self Service*, *Dazed & Confused* and *Studio Voice*. She has also collaborated with designer Laurent Fétis, designed record sleeves and posters for DJ Hell and Tahiti 80, worked with fashion designers Anna Sui, Eley Kishimoto and Diesel, and directed videos and films for Futura 2000, M83 and Japanther.

www.romanticsurf.com

◀ **Artwork for an advertising campaign for Swarovski by Elisabeth Arkhipoff**

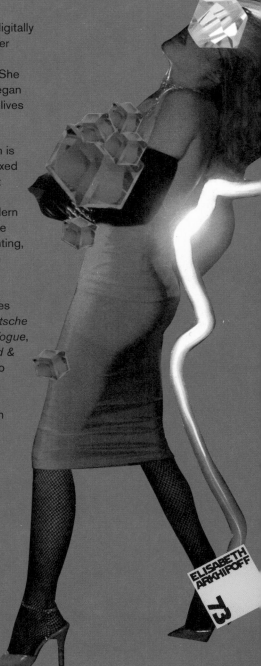

ELISABETH
ARKHIPOFF

73

King Adz vs *Elisabeth Arkhipoff*

When were your formative years?
The 1990s.

Nearest city while growing up?
Paris.

Who, or what, has had an urban influence in the following areas?
MUSIC: *Madness.*
ART: *Andy Warhol.*
DESIGN: *Roger Tallon.*
ADVERTISING/MEDIA: *Decaux.*
FASHION: *Christian Dior.*
FILM: *Martin Scorsese.*
LITERATURE: *Arthur Rimbaud.*
CITY/PLACE: *London.*

How have you made your mark on urban culture?
Via something like Pop art.

What made you realize that urban culture was changing?
When I saw that people were always on their cell phones.

When was that?
A few years ago.

Who should be recognized in this project?
Jean-Michel Basquiat.

What is your favourite food?
Any kind of fruit.

⬥ **Artwork for an advertising campaign for Diesel by Elisabeth Arkhipoff and Laurent Fétis**

PARIS. MONTMARTRE

PARIS

94

DJ Cam

DJ **Cam** is one of my all-time musical heroes. His music has played a massive part in my life and so I was stoked when he agreed to jump on board this project. I felt nervous while waiting for him in the studio but as soon as he walked into the room, shook my hand and looked into my eyes, my apprehension vanished. He is as cool as his music.

DJ Cam invented blunted French instrumental hip hop (or French trip hop) in his seminal album *Underground Vibes*, released in 1994. Together with his follow-up album *Substances* in 1996 (in which he used jazz, blues, world music samples and vocals), DJ Cam changed the face of hip hop in France and took this genre in a completely new direction.

He has collaborated with many US rappers, including J Dilla, Guru, Fank n Dank, Buckshot and MC Eiht, and has also remixed tracks for artists as diverse as Miles Davis and Serge Gainsbourg. He is still producing killer tracks (check out his Bouncer Crew project) and has spoken about the idea of returning to his roots to produce *Substances* parts two, three, four and five.

www.inflamable.com

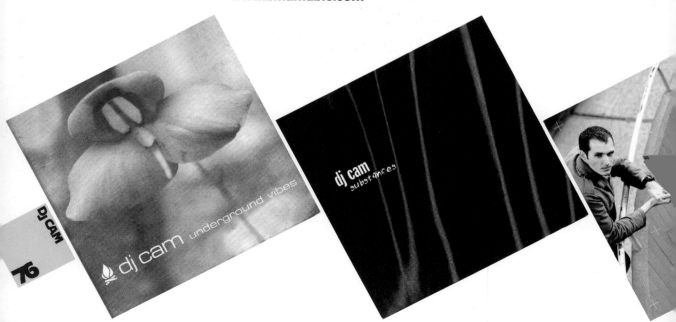

DJ CAM

78

King Adz vs **DJ Cam**

When were your formative years?
From 1973 onwards.

Nearest city while growing up?
Paris.

Who, or what, has had an urban influence in the following areas?
MUSIC: *DJ Premier.*
ART: *Futura 2000.*
DESIGN: *Jean Prouvé.*
ADVERTISING/MEDIA: *Everything.*
FASHION: *Everything.*
FILM: Star Wars.
LITERATURE: *Oscar Wilde.*
CITY/PLACE: *New York and Paris.*

How have you made your mark on urban culture?
I make music, I release records both on my label and on other 'big' labels and I play in many different cities around the world.

What made you realize that urban culture was changing?
When I looked at young kids in the streets and when I watched TV.

When was that?
Every day. Everything is changing so fast.

Who should be recognized in this project?
Charles and Ray Eames.

What is your favourite food?
Thai coconut chicken with sticky rice.

How to make a classic record
by DJ Cam

Main ingredients

My main influences are hip hop, jazz, funk and soul, but I am really, really open-minded. I began collecting records as a child and my parents were shocked when I became a music addict at a young age. I started to DJ at 15 and turned professional at 18: I was fascinated by the whole DJ and hip hop culture. I bought a sampler – an Ensoniq ASR-10 – started to make music and started my own label. I was influenced by DJ Premier, Miles Davis, Bob Marley, Futura 2000, Picasso and Van Gogh. I even moved to New York because I needed to see what the city of hip hop was really like.

Instructions

My first LP (*Underground Vibes*) was a bit special because there wasn't any trip hop in 1994 (except for DJ Shadow and DJ Krush's work). I wanted to make a hip hop LP with an American MC, but I was young and had no money so I decided to make an instrumental hip hop LP without a rapper and use samples instead of MCs. I was at business school at the time and realized that if there were no lyrics people could imagine whatever they wanted within the tunes and I could therefore sell my music anywhere in the world. I was fascinated by the whole concept of a soundtrack and so I threw everything I had into creating something totally new and fresh. I could do anything I wanted. For my second LP it was a little bit different.

When I create music it is an impulsive, almost instinctive, process that comes straight from the heart. I make some music, lay a lot of tracks and let it flow through me. Afterwards I listen to the tracks and work out what to do with the record as a whole and where I really want it to go. I have my own studio at home, and I work from eleven in the morning to six or seven in the evening. I don't work at night, as I prefer to work with the sun.

JR

JR's artivism confronts and provokes Parisians with his outdoor exhibitions which most people get to see on their daily commute to work and back. He is an autodidact, and through his work as an undercover street photographer, JR has transformed his pictures into posters, thereby turning city streets into photo galleries. He is an acute observer of our times and is just as comfortable shooting in chi-chi neighbourhoods as he is in urban ghettoes. Instead of an interview, JR talks to us freely about his life and work in Paris.

www.jr-art.net

I am 25 years old and I own the biggest art gallery in the world. I exhibit freely in the streets, catching the attention of people who are not typical museum visitors. My work talks about commitment, beauty, freedom, identity and limitations.

I started documenting European street art in 1999 after finding a camera in the Paris Métro. I tracked artists who sent messages to each other via their tags and art. Then, I started watching people and the scenes they created from the forbidden areas underground and on the rooftops of the capital.

Later on I created portraits of suburban freaks and posted them in the bourgeois districts of Paris. These photos are taken as close-up shots with a 28-millimetre lens but I blow them up so they can be posted as huge works of art. I use black and white to differentiate my images from aggressive colour advertising. This illegal project became official when the Hôtel de Ville and the Maison Européenne de la Photographie in Paris wrapped their buildings with my photos.

In March 2007 I created the biggest ever illegal photo exhibition with fellow artist Marco. As part of 'Face2Face' we posted my huge portraits of Israelis and Palestinians literally face to face in eight Palestinian and Israeli cities, and on both sides of the security wall that separates them. Everyone thought that people would refuse to pose for the portraits or be posted on the walls, and that the Palestinian police, the Israeli army and the extremists would stop us. But that never happened and we posted more than 4,500 square metres of portraits without any major trouble.

I aim to post my portraits where they make the most sense. I hope that the real surprise of my work is to be surprised by something that is not surprising in itself, such as looking at portraits of yourself, your neighbour or your enemy. Perhaps then we can revisit our prejudices and free ourselves from always thinking in terms of stereotypes. This is what I am working on – raising questions.

◆◆ A portrait by JR from the series '28 Millimetres'

◆ Portrait of Ladj Ly from the series '28 Millimetres'

◆ Installation of 'Portrait of a Generation' in Stolkholm, 2006

◆ Removing photographs from the walls of an outdoor exhibition in Paris, 2006

JR
83

Pleix

My mate Charlotte introduced me to Pleix on the internet (a lot of people have discovered them this way) and to say I was blown away would be an understatement. I'm always on the lookout for progressive film and motion graphics but nothing so far has ever impressed me as much as Pleix's work.

Pleix is a virtual community of filmmakers, musicians, graphic designers and 3D and digital artists based in Paris. Forget everything you know about film and design – Pleix's radical perspective make everything they do totally unique: they craft eloquent, electronic/futuristic imagery and they have produced short films, music videos and mind-blowing commercials. While hanging out with them in Paris, I learned that they like to alternate between working on commercial projects and art films, which is a cool way to work in this day of client-led advertising.

www.pleix.net

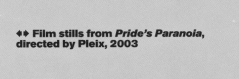

◀▶ **Film stills from *Pride's Paranoia*, directed by Pleix, 2003**

PLEIX

King Adz vs *Pleix*

When were your formative years?
2001.

Nearest city while growing up?
Paris.

Who, or what, has had an urban influence in the following areas?
MUSIC: *Warp Records.*
ART: *Marcel Duchamp.*
DESIGN: *Le Corbusier.*
ADVERTISING/MEDIA: *Michel Gondry.*
FASHION: *No one.*
FILM: *Alfred Hitchcock.*
LITERATURE: *Epicurus (an ancient Greek philosopher).*
CITY/PLACE: *The whole world.*

How have you made your mark on urban culture?
Because it became very easy to make 'new images' with a computer, digital art today is often seen as artificial, cold, devoid of emotion or meaning and spoiled by too many special effects. We try to break the rules by slowing everything down, and we tend to use our digital brains in an organic way. Because advertisers like to make fast-paced animations, and video games seek to satisfy with immediate pleasure, we want to break the youth trend for consuming 'arcade' digital work by using emotional content to educate visually.

◥◥ **Film stills from *Birds*, directed by Pleix, 2006**
◤◤ **Film stills from *Bleip: Clicks*, directed by Pleix, 2003**

PLEIX

89

How to make an original film
by Pleix

1 Find an idea.
2 Find the best ingredients.
3 Experiment with different combinations.
4 Try out the first dish on friends.
5 Don't cook too slowly or too fast.
6 Fine tune.
7 Serve hot.
8 Remember that you can drink wine during the process.
9 Here's an example:

Title: *Sometimes*
Length: 3'02"
Music: by Kid606 / Mille Plateaux Records (2003)

Above all, *Sometimes* (www.pleix.net/films) is a film about dynamism, energy and destruction. The project was inspired by the horrible events of 9/11, but it is also about an explosive scene in Michelangelo Antonioni's film *Zabriskie Point* (1970). We didn't want to make a political point with this project: our analysis is simply to underline the fact that there is physical evolution from all forms of destruction.

➡ **Film still from *Sometimes*, directed by Pleix, 2003**

PLEIX
91

13ᵉ Arrᵗ

RUE
ÉMILE
DURKHEIM
1858 - 1917
SOCIOLOGUE FRANÇAIS

INVADER
92

Invader

Invader has become one of the best-known names in street art, and certainly the most famous in France. His work is everywhere you look in Paris and I lost count of how many pieces I clocked on my journey around the city. So far he has successfully invaded over thirty-five countries with his mosaics of space invaders, Pacman, Mario, Rubik's Cube sculptures, Dig Dug, R2D2, Lou Reed and smiley faces. He has even produced a special sneaker that leaves behind a space invader print as you walk.

Invader began his mission during the early 1990s by putting small colourful mosaic tiles of characters from Toshiro Nishikado's 1978 Space Invaders arcade game around Paris. After a brief stint with pasting up black-and-white posters, he returned to the tiles because they suggested a pixelated old school, low-res video game and the colours made them stand out clearly.

Invader wanted to be represented by his images alone, and so his answers to the cultural influence questionnaire are provided here in picture form.

www.space-invaders.com

BOULEVARD
DE LA
CHAPELLE

INVADER

CHARCUTERI

CUISINE

Mia's SPARE RIBS
96

Mia's spare ribs

The real street food. The French like their pork and I reckon these puppies are the tastiest way to marinate and eat pork. I had some spare ribs at a street grill in Belleville Park and when I got home I called up my mate Mia to tell her all about it. She ended up giving me her version of her granny's recipe.

Feeds 4

1kg/2½ lb **pork spare ribs, separated**

Marinade

4 tablespoons **tomato ketchup**
4 tablespoons **honey**
4 tablespoons **brown vinegar**
1 teaspoon **chilli sauce**
2 tablespoons **soy sauce**
1 **clove garlic, chopped**
1 **lump fresh root ginger, chopped**
75ml/⅓ cup **sherry**

- Combine all the marinade ingredients in a large bowl. Mix well and then stir in the spare ribs one at a time. Marinate for at least 2 hours (overnight is best).

- Cook on a BBQ until done, or bake in the oven for 1 hour at 200°C/400°F/Gas 6 if you can't cook over a real flame.

Mia's
SPARE
RIBS
9

Deep-fried chicken wings in oyster sauce

A killer Chinese dish straight from the streets of Belleville.

Feeds 4

1kg/35oz **chicken wings, chopped into 3
(discard the tips)**
vegetable oil for deep-frying
225ml/8fl oz/1 cup **oyster sauce (can be
bought from Chinese supermarkets)**
2 tablespoons **groundnut oil**

- Deep-fry the chicken wings in hot vegetable oil for 10–20 minutes until they are crisp and brown. Drain, and then transfer them to a separate frying pan.

- Mix together the oyster sauce and groundnut oil, and beat well. Pour this mixture over the chicken wings and mix well in the frying pan over a low heat until all the wings are well covered with sauce and are heated through.

- Serve immediately as a starter.

Spicy hot beef salad

Africa meets uptown Paris in a pavement-café type top-ranking jam/medley of flavours. Hear me now!

Feeds 2

300g/²/₃ lb **beef steak**
  (**fillet, sirloin or rump**)
2 teaspoons **each of ginger and
  garlic pastes**
a good pinch of **peri-peri spice blend**
a splash of **sesame oil**
juice of 1 **lemon**
1 bunch **fresh coriander**
1 **cos or romaine lettuce**
125g/4oz **rocket (arugula) leaves**
2 **tomatoes**
½ **cucumber**
8 **radishes**
a handful each of **salad cress and
  watercress**

• Chop the steak into thin strips and marinate in a mixture of the ginger and garlic pastes, peri-peri spice blend, sesame oil and lemon juice, all to taste, and half the fresh coriander.

• Prepare a regular salad from the rest of the ingredients.

• Heat a little more sesame oil in a frying pan or wok and flash-fry the steak for 5 minutes.

• Add a splash of water and cook for another minute, then put the meat on top of the salad and pour the juices over the whole lot.

SPICY HOT
BEEF SALAD

99

Couscous

Feeds 4

1 **onion, finely chopped**
1 tablespoon **vegetable oil**
4 **chicken portions (chop breasts
  into quarters or use whole thighs,
  or Quorn for a veggie option)**
2 teaspoons **ground cumin**
3 teaspoons **ground allspice**
3 pieces **cinnamon stick**
4 **cloves garlic, chopped**
600ml/1 pint/2¼ cups **chicken or
  vegetable stock**
1 can **tomatoes**
1 can **chickpeas**
juice of 1 **lemon**
20 **green beans**
4 **sticks celery, chopped**
2 **carrots, chopped**
1 **bunch fresh coriander**

Couscous

175g/6oz **couscous**
300ml/10fl oz **boiling water**
a dash **of olive oil**
salt and black pepper

*Although it is originally from the Middle East and
North Africa, couscous is now massive in France,
especially in Paris.*

- Fry the chopped onion for 5 minutes in the vegetable oil.
  Add the chicken or Quorn pieces and fry for a further
  5 minutes. Add all the spices and the garlic and cook on
  a low heat for 5–10 minutes.

- Then add the stock, tomatoes, chickpeas, lemon juice,
  green beans, celery and carrots and simmer for an hour.
  Add more stock if necessary.

- Meanwhile add boiling water to the couscous (follow the
  instructions on the packet). Dribble a dash of olive oil on
  top of the water, cover and cook gently in a low oven, on
  a low setting in the microwave, or on top of the stove for
  about 5 minutes, allowing the couscous to steam gently
  while still covered. When you are ready to serve with the
  sauce, fluff the grains with a fork and season to taste.
  (For added flavour, you can use chicken or vegetable
  stock instead of water when cooking the couscous.)

- Serve the sauce on top of a bed of couscous, sprinkled
  with the fresh coriander.

COUSCOUS - TAGINE

CRAB and SWEETCORN SOUP

Crab and sweetcorn soup

This is a classic Chinese dish that you'll find in most Chinese restaurants around the world, and the predominantly Chinese area of Belleville is no exception. I had a couple of great Chinese meals whilst visiting the La Forge artist studios in Belleville. This is very easy to make and tastes authentic too.

Feeds 2
250g/9oz **crabsticks**
475ml/17fl oz/ a generous 2 cups **chicken or beef stock**
1 can **sweetcorn, drained**
2 **egg whites**
soy sauce
4 teaspoons **cornflour mixed with**
1 teaspoon **water to a thin paste**

- Chop the crabsticks into 1cm/½in chunks.

- Put the stock in a medium pan and bring to the boil. Add the crabsticks and sweetcorn, and heat for 5 minutes.

- Now add the egg whites – make sure you stir the mixture a lot for thin egg wisps or just a little for thick wisps. Add a dash of soy sauce and the cornflour paste, which will thicken the soup. Stir in well, heating gently.

- Serve with more soy sauce.

I got lost between La Chapelle and Montmartre and found a whole street of Moroccan shops and cafés – it was seriously like being in another world. And so after wandering around for a while and passing a couple of cafés with the raddest smells wafting out, I had to stop and eat. This is what I ate.

Ras-el-hanout lamb

Feeds 4

2 tablespoons olive oil

2 **large onions, chopped**

2 **cloves garlic, chopped**

500g/1lb 2oz **lean lamb, cut into bite-sized chunks**

3 teaspoons **ras-el-hanout spice blend (or see note)**

salt and black pepper

475ml/17fl oz/a generous 2 cups **lamb stock**

2 teaspoons **honey**

25g/2 tablespoons **raisins, plumped up in warm water**

100g/1 cup **green beans, sliced**

30g/⅓ cup **sliced almonds, toasted**

- Heat the oil in a large saucepan or deep-sided frying pan and fry the onion and garlic until brown. Remove from the pan and set aside. Fry the lamb in the same pan until browned and then return the onion and garlic. Add the ras-el-hanout and salt and pepper, and stir well to coat the meat.

- Add the stock and bring to the boil, then reduce to a simmer and cook for 1½ hours.

- Then add the honey, drained raisins and green beans, and continue to cook for 30 minutes until the lamb is very tender.

- Scatter the toasted almonds over the meat and serve with hot pitta bread and hummus.

Note

You could make some ras-el-hanout yourself. Grind together the following spices:

1 **cardamom pod;** 1 **teaspoon mace;** 1 **teaspoon grated nutmeg;** 1 **stick cinnamon;**
1 **teaspoon ground chilli;** 1 **teaspoon ground cumin;** 1 **teaspoon ground ginger;**
1 **teaspoon turmeric;** ¾ **teaspoon freshly ground black pepper;**
½ **teaspoon ground dried coriander;** ½ **teaspoon cayenne pepper;**
½ **teaspoon ground allspice;** ¼ **teaspoon ground cloves.**

شاي رفيع مستورد من سيلان

IMPORTATION & DISTRIBUTION

Omrane
produits de qualité

Savourez le meilleur du Couscous

01 40 36 05 31   01 40 36 10 07
www.omrane.com

Conrad's chicken liver pâté

During my time in Paris I would buy pâté from a deli in the Bastille and eat it spread on French bread from a local bakery, sitting in the street watching the beautiful students and hipsters of Paris's hippest district schlep past. That's living all right!

Feeds 4–6

250g/9oz **frozen chicken livers (keep the pots they are packed in and wash thoroughly)**
1 **small onion, chopped into 4**
3 **cloves garlic**
2 **egg yolks**
a lot of **salt and black pepper**
a splash of **brandy or whisky**
a dash of **cream**
butter

• Cover the livers, onions and garlic with water and simmer for about 20 minutes until cooked.

• Slide the egg yolks into the water while the liquid is simmering to keep them whole.

• When the livers are cooked, pour off the fluid and throw it away. Put the remainder through a mincer or blender. Add plenty of salt and pepper to taste, and more garlic if needed. Then add a splash of brandy or whisky, and a dash of cream. Combine everything well and re-use the thoroughly washed plastic pots to put the pâté in.

• Melt enough butter to cover the top of the pâté. Leave the pâté to cool, then refrigerate and use within a week (although this pâté can be frozen). Serve spread on hot toast with black pepper and fresh lemon juice.

Biryani

This recipe is in honour of the Café Bharath (see Hit List, p. 69) that sorted me out with the best Indian food and endless cups of cardamon chai almost every day of my stay in Paris.

Feeds 6–8

3 tablespoons **tomato purée**

200g/7oz **plain yoghurt**

1 **teaspoon each of ginger and garlic pastes**

1 **green chilli, chopped**

1 teaspoon **each of red chilli powder, turmeric and ground cumin**

2 teaspoons **each of garam masala and ground coriander**

salt to taste

1 kg/2¼lb **chicken pieces (or beef or lamb)**

1 teaspoon **vegetable oil**

1 **onion, finely chopped**

300g/11oz **basmati rice**

a pinch of **saffron strands**

100ml/nearly ½ cup **milk**

2 **cardamom pods**

1 bunch **fresh coriander**

4 **hard-boiled eggs, shelled and halved**

- Mix together the tomato purée, yoghurt, ginger and garlic pastes, green chilli, all the ground spices and salt in a bowl. Marinate the chicken in this mixture for 3–4 hours.

- Heat the oil in a pan and fry the onion until golden brown. Remove the chicken pieces from the marinade, add to the pan and cook for 15 minutes.

- Wash the rice and add enough water to cover it by 1cm/½in. Mix the saffron with the milk and add to the rice, along with the whole cardamom pods. Add the chicken pieces and the remainder of the marinade. Bring the rice to the boil, cover with a tight lid and cook for 20 minutes.

- Turn off the heat and allow to stand for 5–10 minutes (depending on how hungry you are!).

- When the rice is ready, mix gently and garnish with the fresh coriander. Serve with boiled egg halves on top.

EAST SIDE
GALLERY

World

Hier erlebt Berlin.

"Berlin has so much to offer: there are loads of budget airlines flying into the three airports in and around the city, tons of decent hostels and budget hotels to stay in, and lots and lots of events, gigs and venues to check out. Moreover, the city is full of youthful people with time on their hands and not much money to spend, and so everything is incredibly cheap and accessible."

Because there is so much going on in **Berlin**, I am only going to focus on the areas in and around Kreuzberg. I stayed there in the fantastic Die Fabrik hostel (see Hit List), which is a converted old factory only a short walk from Schlesisches Tor U-Bahn station, and just across the river from a section of the Berlin Wall that is still standing. Be sure to check out the open-air art there at the East Side Gallery. This is as deep as the history lesson gets, though – there isn't much left of the wall…

However, there is a whole world waiting to be explored behind Berlin's other walls: if you get the chance it is worth checking out the many courtyards (most of which are accessible to the public) tucked away behind the tall buildings all round the city. Even if you are walking along the most urban of streets, you need only step through a graffiti-clad archway into another dimension: ponds, trees, artists' studios, kindergartens, communal eating, living spaces and cinemas… Berlin courtyards boast them all.

Kreuzberg and Friedrichshain

Immediately on arrival in Berlin I spent six hours walking around the Kreuzberg area, and came to the conclusion that it is one the dopest places I've ever visited. It has the best quality and highest abundance of street art, dozens of cool pavement cafés and bars, and loads of people sitting around in groups in parks and on pavements just chilling and chatting. Good vibes all round.

Kreuzberg street life is massive: people cycle everywhere on a wicked system of cycle paths, and it has more indie shops, restaurants, venues and bars than you can possibly ever visit in one trip. It also has a large Turkish population with great kebab shops and cafés surrounded by kids playing in the side streets, mothers and grannies chatting to one another and teenage girls talking on cell phones.

Check out Görlitzer Park – it's mad at night, with popular drinking haunts on the left and north west side. Or bring a BBQ to the park at the weekend and spend the day cooking and chilling there with other Berlin urbanites. Kreuzberg was once known as the squatter and counter-culture centre of West Berlin, and this spirit is still heavily in the air: a riot is planned every 1 May, and for the rest of the year the protests are mainly against capitalism and consumerism.

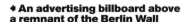
◆ An advertising billboard above a remnant of the Berlin Wall

BERLIN
113

The Kunstraum Kreuzberg/Bethanien (see the Hit List) is an old Gothic hospital that was saved from demolition in the 1970s and is now used for cultural and artistic purposes. During the summer months, various Kreuzberg festivals are held in or around the Kunstraum, and an open-air cinema is erected there too.

Just across the river from Kreuzberg is Friedrichshain – another great neighbourhood that used to be on the border between East and West. In recent years it has become a haven for young artists, designers and students who want to live and work in affordable spaces, and there are plenty of cheap, unpretentious bars and cafés on and around the Simon-Dach-Strasse, Boxhagener Strasse and Wühlischstrasse. I ate a traditional German meal in Schneeweiss (see the Hit List) with photographer Martin Eberle (see p. 120) and mooched out over a pizza from Steinofen on Falckensteinstrasse (see Hit List). Surrounded by incredibly friendly people on a warm Sunday evening in June, I even went over the top and bought an ice cream sundae from the booth opposite the pizza joint. Life on the edge – hey!

Backjumps Live

Backjumps Live is an annual international festival held in Berlin to showcase urban communication and aesthetics, and street art too. As the name suggests, this project transforms Berlin into a live issue of *Backjumps* magazine (www.backjumps. org) with its exhibitions, parties, workshops, walks, movies, public-space activities and urban events. Backjumps Live is Berlin's way of proving that street art is more than just mindless scribbling. By proving that it contributes to the public's perception of art, advertising and culture, street art can be appreciated as an art form worthy of serious consideration and critical discussion.

So who better to hook up with during the festival than New York artist Brad Downey. Brad is best known for being one half of street artist team Darius & Downey who make street sculptures from furniture found on the streets of New York. Brad also directed *Public Discourse* – a film about illegal installation art, the painting of street signs, advertising manipulation, postering and guerrilla art. We entered into the street spirit of things by spending a night surrounded by Berliners just sitting, chilling and chatting about street art on a bit of wasteland by the river.

▶ **A view of the Kreuzberg area of Berlin from the U-Bahn**

Hit List

Food

Ice Cream Booth
Falckensteinstrasse (opposite Steinofen Pizza)

King Köfte
Wrangelstrasse

Schneeweiss
Simplonstrasse 16

Steinofen Pizza
Falckensteinstrasse 6

West Side Kebabs
Schlesische Strasse 10

White Trash Fast Food
Schönhauser Allee 8

Bar/club

Yaam am Ostbahnhof
Stralauer Platz 35

Accommodation

Die Fabrik
Schlesische Strasse 18

Venues/entertainment/museums

Eiszeit Kino
Zeughofstrasse 20 (cinema)

Kunstraum Kreuzberg/Bethanien
Mariannenplatz 2 (museum)

Lido
Schlesische Strasse/Cuvrystrasse 7

Shopping

BackYard
2nd Backyard, Rosenthaler Strasse 39,
(a community of artist studios, a small
cinema, a cocktail bar, the Neurotitan
art gallery and a shop)

Granatengarten
Falckensteinstrasse 4 (Fashion)

Hip Hop Stützpunkt
Marienburger Strasse 16 (hip hop arts centre)

My iPod Playlist

Zbigniew Preisner
Preisner's Music

Smashing Pumpkins
Adore

DJ Cam
Underground Vibes (see p. 76)

Skinnyman
'I'll be Surprised'

Manic Street Preachers
This Is My Truth Tell Me Yours

Maria Callas
The Voice of the Century

DJ Premier
Signature Sounds Vol. 1

Marvin Gaye
'"T" Plays it Cool'

Sigur Rós
Hlemmur

David Bowie
Heroes

➧ **The shop window at Granatengarten, an
art gallery and boutique in the Kreuzberg
neighbourhood in Berlin**

FRIEND OF THE WEEK

dolores★

rosa - luxemburg - str.7 / berlin mitte
Tel.:030 / 280 99 597
Steuernummer 11 34 395 53339
****

Nr.: 107

Coke	1,50 €
Lime Chicken	4,25 €
Black Beans	
Red Chili	
Saure Sahne	

Saldo	5,75 €
Nettoumsatz	4,83 €
MwSt 19%	0,92 €
Bar	5,75 €
07.06.07 1 Chef	107

Nachdruck verboten

↑ Bitte hier entwerten
Please validate your ticket

Tageskarte
Regeltarif

Berlin AB
B1T   6,10 EUR
080607 0853   01321

Gemeinsamer Tarif der im Verkehrsverbund Berlin-Brandenburg
zusammenwirkenden Verkehrsunternehmen (VBB-Tarif).
Gültig nach den geltenden Beförderungsbedingungen.
BVG · Potsdamer Straße 188 · 10783 Berlin · Tel. 2560.

55140 1991   BVG

m-city.org

ALIAS

WATERGATE
02.06.07
23.00H

TRAILERPARK
BERLIN

BERLIN
119

Martin Eberle

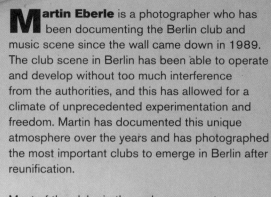

Martin Eberle is a photographer who has been documenting the Berlin club and music scene since the wall came down in 1989. The club scene in Berlin has been able to operate and develop without too much interference from the authorities, and this has allowed for a climate of unprecedented experimentation and freedom. Martin has documented this unique atmosphere over the years and has photographed the most important clubs to emerge in Berlin after reunification.

Most of the clubs in the early years post-reunification were located in Berlin-Mitte, the former East Germany, or in the wasteland between East and West, and included Tresor, e-werk, WMF 1 and Elektro. But as the scene evolved, more clubs opened in the area around Hackescher Markt (WMF 4–6, galerie berlintokyo, Kunst + Technik, Eimer and Junk). Martin's book *Temporary Spaces*, published in 2001, showed pictures of twenty-eight of these clubs.

www.craenkl.de

MARTIN
EBERLE
121

King Adz vs *Martin Eberle*

When were your formative years?
Probably while studying at the University of Applied Sciences, Dortmund from 1987 to 1992, and between 1996 and 1999 while I was working with galerie berlintokyo. Both experiences laid the foundation of my interest in cultural and media practice.

Nearest city while growing up?
Ulm/Donau in Germany.

Who, or what, has had an urban influence in the following areas?
MUSIC: *Grateful Dead, Patti Smith, Sonic Youth, Bob Mould, Spacemen 3, Spiritualized, Marusha, Ellen Alien, WestBam, Aphex Twin, Aimee Mann, Maria Callas, Ryuichi Sakamoto, Jeans Team and Milch.*
ART: *Joseph Beuys, Jeff Koons, Franz Gertsch, Ralph Gibson, Robert Frank, Eugène Atget, Jacques-Henri Lartigue and Todd Hido.*
FASHION: *Donna Karan, Hugo Boss and Helmut Lang.*
FILM: *Rainer Werner Fassbinder, Francis Ford Coppola (Apocalypse Now) and Robert Altman (Short Cuts).*
LITERATURE: *Bret Easton Ellis, Jörg Schröder, Ernst Jünger, Rainald Goetz and Thomas Pynchon.*

How have you made your mark on urban culture?
I try to follow the various phenomena that have influenced my personal life. For example, in the early 1990s the combination of free and available space after the wall came down and the new age of electronic and techno music were fascinating. I began to go to clubs, and then ended up running a club, and all along I was photographing these places. I still photograph the people, mostly musicians who I met ten or fifteen years ago, as the contemporary performers they still are today.

What made you realize that urban culture was changing?
Culture is changing all the time. It is more interesting to establish which part of the development of cultural history you have taken part in before the next generation of people takes over.

When was that?
11 May 1996.

Who should be recognized in this project?
Heinrich Dubel (www.erratik-institut.de) and Sabine Reinfeld (www.frauberlin.com).

What is your favourite food?
When I cook I prefer to roast things like deer, rabbit or lamb.

◆◆ **Photograph by Martin Eberle of galerie berlintokyo**
◆ **Musician Annika Line Trost, photographed by Martin Eberle**

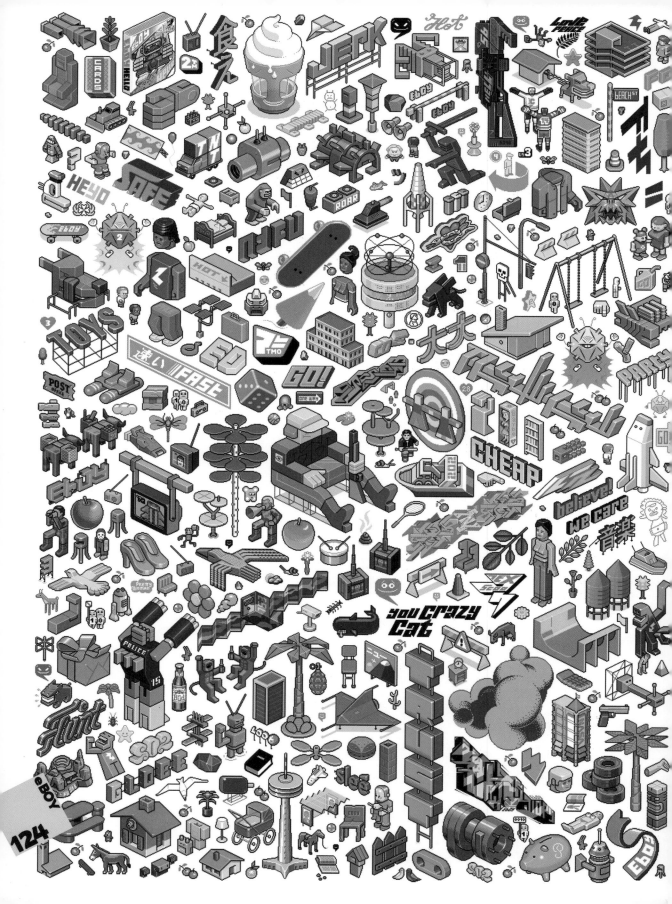

eBoy

eBoy is formed of graphic artists Svend Smital, Steffen Sauerteig and Kai Vermehr, who together are the collective gods of their amazing, colourful and pixelated world. Inspired by popular culture, they produce unique and original illustrations, web designs, fonts and games, and have quickly built up an international cult following.

www.eboy.com

King Adz vs eBoy

When were your formative years?
1998.

Nearest cities while growing up?
Berlin, Caracas, Frankfurt and Guatemala City.

Who, or what, has had an urban influence in the following areas?
MUSIC: *Suicide and The Stooges.*
ART: *Andy Warhol and Keith Haring.*
ADVERTISING/MEDIA: *The Designers Republic, Cornel Windlin, The Face and i-D Magazine.*
FASHION: *Vivienne Westwood, Levi's®, vintage, jail and army clothing, and Maharishi.*
FILM: *Taxi Driver.*
LITERATURE: *Neal Stephenson's Snow Crash.*
CITY/PLACE: *New York.*

How have you made your mark on urban culture?
By squeezing everything into small square boxes.

What made you realize that urban culture was changing?
As far as we can tell, everything changes all the time.

When was that?
We can't really tell…

Who should be recognized in this project?
The parka designers from the US army.

What is your favourite food?
A different dish every day.

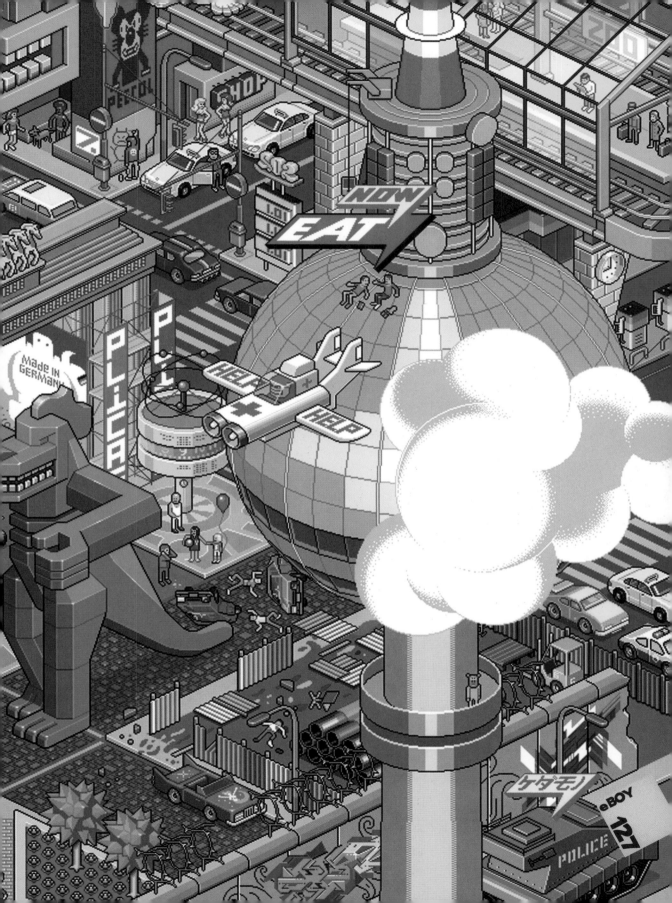

!K7 Records

!K7 Records are a Berlin-based independent record label dedicated to electronic music. Juan Vandervoort is the senior A&R guy there and I hooked up with him on my trip to Berlin. Juan has a great love – and ear – for progressive music, and this is reflected in the many and varied artists who are part of the !K7 label.

!K7 got its first real global props with its now legendary X-MIX DJ mix compilations, with contributions from Laurent Garnier, Richie Hawtin, Ken Ishii, Dave Angel, Kevin Saunderson and Dave Clarke. Then the Rapster Records label was set up in 2001 under the !K7 umbrella, focusing on urban, soul and hip hop records, and it is through this eclecticism that !K7 Records became renowned as one of the most diverse electronic music labels in the world.

www.k7.com
www.everrecords.com
www.rapsterrecords.com
www.dj-kicks.com

➧ **Detail of cover art from the *DJ-Kicks: Four Tet* album released by !K7**

King Adz vs !K7 Records

When were your formative years?
From 1988 to 1998.

Nearest city while growing up?
Brussels.

Who, or what, has had an urban influence in the following areas?
MUSIC: *Disco rap, early 1980s hip hop, electro and early 1990s electronica.*
ART: *Toys"R"Us? Toys r art!*
DESIGN: *Technics SL 1200 turntables, Sony Walkman/Maxell tapes and vocoders.*
ADVERTISING/MEDIA: *Fanzines.*
FASHION: *Pins/badges/buttons. And pin ups, of course.*
FILM: *When pixels kill pixels (film doesn't do much for me. It's not much more than pixels killing pixels most of the time).*
LITERATURE: *Comics and Philip K. Dick.*
CITY/PLACE: *New York and London.*

How have you made your mark on urban culture?
By spreading the news.

What made you realize that urban culture was changing?
When there was any change in music. And music is always changing.

When was that?
Yesterday, today, tomorrow.

Who should be recognized in this project?
Egyptian Lover.

What are your favourite foods?
Sushi and pizza.

DJ CAM
DJ-KICKS:

STEREO MC'S
DJ-KICKS:

tosca
Suzuki

Andrea Parker DJ-KICKS:
Andrea Parker
DJ-KICKS:

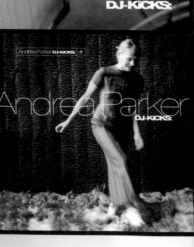

HERBERT

SWAYZAK
Route
de la Slack

PRISM
#1

silver or lead   ★ URSULA RUCKER

DJ-KICKS ★
erlend øye

Henrik Schwarz DJ-KICKS

!K7
RECORDS
131

How to sign talent
by !K7 Records

There are many different ways to discover an act, but it is usually individual artists or managers who get in touch with us. We have A&R people in- and out-of-house who are constantly looking on our behalf. And we have scouts who are not necessarily on the payroll – they might be people who just like the label and tip us off about certain things. There are loads and loads of talents to check on MySpace, and there are people sending in demos and stuff all the time. Basically there's a helluva lot of music out there.

What we don't have at !K7 Records is a preconceived idea of what we like. We are open to everything and we have no agenda and no genres that we stick to.

The first thing that grabs me about a new track or band is my immediate personal reaction to the music. But it's hard to describe exactly why you connect to certain things. It would be easy if you connected to the same things all the time, but you always want to hear something new and it still surprises me when I do. So when I get a reaction I'm the first and last filter, and if I'm working as a part of a team and if something excites me on a personal and professional level, then I check out that excitement with other people.

If the excitement is shared with the rest of the team then the next question is always 'are they a debut act?' If they are then there's a lot of work to be done: getting in touch with the band or their management; discussing how it would work for the band to be part of the label; finding out if the musicians can tour live.

You also need to know that it isn't gonna be a one-off. We don't sign one-hit wonders and we don't do the hype thing either. We want to pick up and support artists whose second and third albums will be just as exciting as their debut albums. But we also want to get an understanding of how an artist will develop, how his or her career will go and whether all that will be good for the label.

We then sign up the act and map out how we would like the band or musician to develop. And then we promote and market them. It's different if you are working with an established artist who comes in with a finished album, but for a debut act the setup times are much longer.

There's a lot of new music out there and it's getting increasingly difficult for debut acts to break through. You have to use all available methods of promotion: touring, music videos, promotional and press strategies, the internet, DJ mailings, radio coverage and magazines. Single methods don't work – you have to connect the dots and then think about merchandizing, and even then there is still no guarantee of success, because you can't force something on anyone. The only thing that can really make an album grow is word of mouth. That's the only thing that really works.

Rinzen

Rinzen is a five-member art, design and illustration collective that started out in their hometown of Brisbane in 2000, but are now based in various locations. Steve and Rilla Alexander have set up their studio in Berlin for easy access to Europe, America and the rest of the world. Craig Redman works from New York, Karl Maier is in Melbourne, and Adrian Clifford holds down the fort in Brisbane.

Rinzen works in all mediums, still and moving, and has gone from strength to strength creating original and outstanding work for such clients as HP, MTV, Puma, VW, VH1, DC Comics, Nylon, Frame and Mooks. Each member has their own unique style, which only becomes apparent in finished design and illustrations. Steve Alexander shares his background with us.

www.rinzen.com

King Adz vs Rinzen

When were your formative years?
From 1973 onwards.

Nearest city while growing up?
For me it was Ipswich, Australia. For the rest of Rinzen it was Brisbane, Rockhampton, the Gold Coast and Coffs Harbour.

How have you made your mark on urban culture?
By painting and drawing. I'm not sure I did anything different to what anyone else was doing, though. I do what I do, I make what I want and I enjoy doing it. Collectively we were focused on making things our own way and not conforming – strength in numbers.

What made you realize that urban culture was changing?
I have been aware for quite some time that culture changes. It never rests. Cultures have shifted from their origins even in the most traditional places – it's entirely natural. Everyone is influenced by things they come into contact with and that shapes what they do. What is culture anyway? For me it's a collection of experiences, expressed through imagery, sounds, movement and the written language.

When was that?
I honestly can't recall the day it happened.

Who should be recognized in this project?
There are so many people making wonderful work at the moment that there are too many to list.

What is your favourite food?
I'm totally into beans at the moment, so feijoada would be the winner (a Brazilian bean stew). I love a good chilli con carne too! Actually, anything Mexican is good. I miss the Mexican restaurant El Torito in West End, Brisbane, Australia. The best Mexican food I've ever eaten.

▶▶ **Design collaboration between Rinzen and photographers Lyn Balzer and Tony Perkins for the publication** *In the Milky Night*, **2006**

RINZEN

136

How to create original designs and illustrations
by Rinzen

From a discusion with
Steve and Rilla Alexander

Experimentation is very important. Sometimes when a design or an illustration style is taken out of context it can lose all meaning, and so our main piece of advice is to always think about the meaning of your designs. Then you should always make sure that the components of that art work actually represent something and work towards making the concept comprehensible. People often forget to include things that have a real purpose, focusing instead on aesthetics. But you need to take your time and think about how to develop things further.

You also need to surround yourself with different cultural influences: you need to travel and find places that inspire you, and you have to get out and meet and speak to people, rather than just opening a book and thinking 'This is the way to go.' You should never develop work directly from design books, but take inspiration from what is around you. It's nice to be inspired by design books and annuals but there's a risk that it has all been done before. A successful design or illustration is about being inspired by other things, but also about creating something that is an inspiration for other people.

Another important part of creativity is simply to draw and think of ideas all the time. So use notebooks. Fill them with ideas. And try to avoid novelty tricks like filters, plug-ins and drop-shadows in your work – they are easy to find and everyone can use them. Having an original idea is the most important thing you can do. And less is always better.

Akim Walta

A **kim** is one of Europe's true hip hop pioneers. He set up the first German hip hop magazine, *Mzee*, as well as the graffiti magazine *On the Run*, and also managed the release of the first German hip hop record in 1992. He then recorded the first German hip hop track 'Breakers Revenge' as Zeb. Rok.Ski with producers/rappers the Stieber Twins in 1993, and in 1995 went on to set up the first German hip hop agency From Here To Fame which publishes books, promotes records, sells mail-order graffiti supplies and offers artist management too.

Most recently, in 2007, Akim opened Hip Hop-Stützpunkt (see the Hit List) – the ultimate in all things hip hop, with an art gallery devoted to graffiti, a recording studio, a production office and a video editing suite with design and production workstations and warehouse storage for products. The idea is that all projects can be created in-house from start to finish, so a DJ can produce a track in the studio and a rapper can then come in and lace the vocals. Meanwhile the video can be shot and edited, a sleeve designed and the press release planned and produced.

www.fromheretofame.com

◄ **A photograph by Martha Copper comes to life in cut-out form**

HIP HOP STÜTZPUNKT

AKIM WALTA 141

King Adz vs *Akim Walta*

When were your formative years?
In 1982 I heard hip hop for the first time; in 1983 I started up a B-boy crew (Supreme Force) and organized hip hop parties. From 1987 until the early 1990s I travelled a lot and joined B-boy circles every weekend. In 1988 I started managing rap crews and promoting rap and hip hop events. I started my own graffiti magazine, On the Run, *in 1990 (the first European graffiti magazine in colour) and built up the Mzee label so that in 1992 I could found Mzee Records and focus on producing German rap. By 2000 I had started to work with Martha Cooper on the coffee-table book* Hip Hop Files *that led me into the world of publishing and inspired me to create a hip hop museum.*

Nearest city while growing up?
Budenheim – a small village near Mainz, Germany.

Who, or what, has had an urban influence in the following areas?
MUSIC: *Bob James, James Brown, Isaac Hayes, Marley Marl, Arthur Baker, Hank Shocklee, DJ Premier, Pete Rock, DJ Red Alert, DJ Chuck Chillout, Tim Westwood and Dee Nasty.*
ART: *Sam Esses, Stefan 1, GPI, Patti Astor, Dondi, Futura 2000 and Vaughn Bode.*
DESIGN: *Haze and Cey One.*
ADVERTISING/MEDIA: *Fab 5 Freddy, Michael Holman and Not From Concentrate.*
MAGAZINES: Village Voice *and* Art Magazine.
FASHION: *The Gangs and creative B-boys of New York City.*
FILM: Style Wars *by Tony Silver and Henry Chalfant,* Wild Style *by Charlie Ahearn and* Beat Street *by Steven Hager.*

LITERATURE: *Subway Art by Martha Cooper and Henry Chalfant,* Getting Up: Subway Graffiti in New York *by Craig Castleman,* The Faith of Graffiti *by Jon Naar and* Hip Hop: The Illustrated History of Break Dancing, Rap Music, and Graffiti *by Steven Hager.*
CITY/PLACE: *New York (Henry Chalfant's studio); Paris (Stalingrad Hall of Fame); Amsterdam (Amstel Station, Hall of Fame); London (Covent Garden writer meetings); Biel (La Couple, Jams); Munich (Berg am Laim, Hip Hop Headquarters); and Heidelberg (at home with the Stieber and Maldonado family).*

How have you made your mark on urban culture?
See above.

What made you realize that urban culture was changing?
When you heard rap on every radio station, saw baggy pants everywhere, watched graffiti in major advertising campaigns and witnessed B-boys taking over on TV. The old-school revival came later on, and the street art boom too.

When was that?
From about 2000 onwards.

Who should be recognized in this project?
There are too many to mention, but these people would definitely be on my list: Seen, Mode 2, the Stieber Twins, Blade, Kane 1 and Wane COD.

What is your favourite food?
Green or red Thai chicken curry.

➔ A graffiti artist painting a canvas at an event at Hip Hop Stützpunkt, Berlin

Sweet and sour fish

As in most cities of the world, Chinese dishes are a popular street food. Berlin has a mental selection of Chinese restaurants and takeaways, and this recipe, adapted from a dish I ate in one of them, will keep you away from the MSG for a while…. This dish can also be made using chicken or prawns.

Feeds 4–6
1kg/2 ¼lb **cod, haddock or salmon**
plain flour
salt and black pepper
vegetable oil, for deep-frying

Batter mix
115g/4oz **plain flour**
55g/2oz **cornflour**
a pinch of **salt**
200ml/7fl oz **cold fizzy soda water**

Sweet and sour sauce
500ml/18fl oz **water**
4 tablespoons **sugar**
2 **carrots, finely sliced**
1 **medium onion, roughly chopped**
3 **peppers (any colour), chopped**
125g/4oz **pineapple chunks, drained
  and chopped**
red colouring
1 tablespoon **cornflour mixed with
  a little water**
4 teaspoons **clear vinegar (distilled
  malt vinegar)**

- Make the sweet and sour sauce first. Put the water and sugar in a medium pan and heat until dissolved. In another pan, lightly cook the carrots in boiling water, then drain and add to the water and sugar mixture. Add the remaining vegetables, pineapple and red colouring to the sauce.

- Use the cornflour mixture to thicken the sauce. At this point it should be thicker than you want it to be at the end. Remove the pan from the heat and stir well as you add the vinegar. Leave to one side, and warm through briefly when serving.

- Whisk all the batter ingredients together until light and fluffy. The mixture should be fairly thick and leave a trail when the whisk is lifted out of the batter.

- Cut the fish into bite-sized pieces and toss in seasoned flour. Dip the fish into the batter and fry in hot oil in a deep frying pan until golden brown and crisp, about 5 minutes. Drain on a paper towel.

- Serve the battered fish on top of boiled rice, covered with sweet and sour sauce.

Hansa salmon

Named after the legendary West Berlin recording studio where David Bowie, Lou Reed and a load of other big names recorded seminal albums in the 1970s and early 1980s.

Feeds 2–4
2–4 **salmon fillets**
3 **teaspoons garlic paste from a jar**
½ **jar pepperdew peppers**
200g/7oz **green beans**
20 **black olives, pitted**
6 **tomatoes, quartered**
25ml/1fl oz **lemon juice**
peri-peri spice blend (optional)
1 small can **anchovies**

- Wash and place the salmon fillets in an ovenproof dish. Spread the garlic paste over the top of the fish. Surround the salmon in the dish with the pepperdews, green beans, olives and tomatoes.

- Add half of the lemon juice and some peri-peri spice blend to taste (optional). Place two anchovies across each piece of salmon.

- Cook in the oven at 200°C/400°F/Gas 6 for 20 minutes.

- Douse with the remaining lemon juice, and serve with rice or noodles.

Spinach dhal

I had a few good curries in Berlin, but the best Indian dish I ate was a simple vegetarian dhal from a takeaway kiosk in the Friedrichshain area.

Feeds 4–6
250g/9oz **chana dhal lentils**
1 **onion, chopped**
1 tablespoon **vegetable oil**
2 teaspoons **turmeric**
2 teaspoons **ground cumin**
1 teaspoon **ground coriander**
5 **curry leaves**
4 teaspoons **each of ginger and garlic pastes from a jar**
4 **large tomatoes, quartered**
300g/11oz **washed spinach**
½ **cauliflower, broken into florets**
1 **chicken or vegetable stock cube,** dissolved in 400ml/14fl oz/1¾ cups **water**
2 **chillies (red and green), chopped**
125g/4oz **yoghurt**
1 teaspoon **garam masala**
1 bunch **fresh coriander, chopped**

- Soak the dhal in water for a few hours and then simmer for a couple of hours.

- In a deep pan, fry the chopped onion in the oil until it is golden brown and almost burnt.

- Then add the cooked dhal, spices, curry leaves, ginger and garlic pastes, and cook for 10 minutes.

- Add the tomatoes, spinach, cauliflower, stock and chillies and then cook for an hour on a low heat, adding water if necessary.

- Add the yoghurt and garam masala, and sprinkle with freshly chopped coriander when you are ready to eat. Serve with basmati rice and pickles.

Kedgeree

A German breakfast special. But I like it a bit later in the day! Really easy to make – it should take less than half an hour.

Feeds 4
200g/7oz **basmati rice**
a tablespoon of butter
250g/9oz **smoked mackerel or herring**
  (remove the skin)
300g/2 cups **frozen peas**
4 **hard-boiled eggs, shelled**
  and quartered
soy sauce
salt and black pepper
chilli oil (optional)

• Wash and soak the rice, then add enough salted water to cover the rice by 1cm/½in, bung on a lid and bring to the boil. As soon as the water reaches boiling point, reduce to the lowest heat possible and cook gently for 20 minutes before removing from the stove. Drain.

• Melt the butter and cook the fish in a large frying pan or wok for at least 5 minutes, breaking it up into small pieces. Add the cooked rice and mix well. Then add the peas and the hard-boiled eggs.

• Fry the whole mixture for about 5 minutes until it begins to stick to the pan. Add a splash of soy sauce, and season to taste with salt and black pepper.

• Serve with more soy sauce and chilli oil (optional).

Kofta

This recipe if dedicated to Brad Downey who hooked me up with a great kofta takeaway in Kreutzberg – they really know about Turkish kebabs there. You will need ten skewers.

Feeds 5

500g/1lb 2oz **minced ground beef steak**

1 **small onion, grated**

4 teaspoons **garlic paste from a jar**

3 tablespoons **chopped fresh flat-leaf parsley**

2 tablespoons **chopped fresh coriander**

1 tablespoon **ground coriander**

1 teaspoon **each of ground cumin and chilli powder**

½ teaspoon **each of ground cinnamon and ground allspice**

¼ teaspoon **each of cayenne pepper and ground ginger**

salt and black pepper

2 teaspoons **olive oil**

1 tablespoon **lemon juice**

- Mix all the ingredients together in a large bowl and leave for about an hour.

- Divide into ten round balls and then roll out into sausage shapes. Skewer each sausage and then grill, or BBQ (my preference).

- Serve with rice or in toasted pitta bread with salad.

Chicken chips

This street food recipe is originally from Guyana, but the guy who showed me how to cook chicken chips ended up living in Berlin. I was living in Brighton and first discovered the dish when my Guyanese mate came to stay for the weekend and showed me how to make it. So there you go, the complete story of the travels of chicken chips! From Guyana to London to Brighton to Berlin…

Feeds 2 as a snack
3 **chicken breast fillets**
1 **egg**
140g/5oz **plain flour**
salt and black pepper
2 teaspoons **cayenne pepper or peri-peri**
spice blend
cooking oil

- Wash and cut the chicken into chip-sized pieces. Beat the egg in a bowl. Bung the chicken into the egg, making sure each piece is well coated.

- Mix the flour, salt, pepper and cayenne pepper in another bowl and dip each piece of chicken into it, thoroughly coating the meat.

- Half-fill a large pan with cooking oil and put on a high heat. After 5 minutes (or when the oil is very hot), place the pieces of coated chicken into the pan of oil and turn down the heat to medium.

- Cook until the chicken is golden brown, about 10 minutes.

- Drain, place on paper towel to dry, and then serve as a starter with a sweet chilli dip and/or mayonnaise.

Trinchada

I bought this dish from a crazy food stall (actually an old caravan) on a visit to a street festival held in June around the Kunstraum museum and park. It's from Portugal originally but the recipe has mutated into something very Eurocentric.

Feeds 2

1 tablespoon **unsalted butter**
1 tablespoon **olive oil**
675g/1½lb **rump steak, cut into small cubes**
1 **large onion, chopped**
3 or 4 **small hot red chilli peppers, chopped**
4 **cloves garlic, chopped**
725ml/scant 1¼ pints/3 cups **beef stock**
½ **bottle red wine**
1 **bay leaf**
1 jar/can **black olives, or a couple of good handfuls**
salt and black pepper

• Heat a large pan over a medium-high heat for 2 minutes. Add the butter and oil. Once the butter is melted, add the beef cubes a few at a time and brown well on all sides. Don't cook too many cubes at once, crowd the pan or rush this step: this is what gives the dish its flavour. Remove the cooked cubes and leave to one side on a plate.

• Lower the heat to medium, add the onion and chilli and cook until softened, about 10 minutes.

• Add the garlic and cook for 1 more minute. Pour in the stock and red wine. Stir until the sauce thickens a bit, about 3 minutes. Then add the bay leaf, olives, browned beef cubes and any juices that may have accumulated on the plate. Bring to the boil, reduce the heat to low and simmer, covered, for about 2 hours. Season to taste with salt and black pepper.

• Serve with lots of crustry French bread for dunking.

TRINCHADA

Beef stroganoff

An old-school Germanic classic. This one is for the good ol' German boys I got down with one lazy Sunday Berlin morning.

Feeds 4
500g/1lb 2oz **good quality steak**
55g/2oz **butter**
1 **onion, finely chopped**
black pepper
1 **tablespoon dried basil**
1 **teaspoon paprika**
a splash **of Worcestershire sauce**
a splash **of cooking sherry or red wine**
½ teaspoon **freshly grated nutmeg**
475ml/17fl oz/generous 2 cups **beef stock**
4 teaspoons **cornflour, mixed**
  with 1 teaspoon **water to a thin paste**
375g/13oz **egg noodles**
200g/7oz **button mushrooms, sliced**
150ml/5oz **sour cream**

- Cut the steak into long narrow strips and cook in butter until brown in a frying pan. Add the chopped onion to the meat and cook for a couple of minutes. Add some black pepper, the basil, paprika, Worcestershire sauce, cooking sherry or red wine, nutmeg and beef stock, and simmer on a very low heat for at least an hour. Check regularly and add more water if needed. Thicken the sauce with the cornflour mixture.

- Meanwhile, cook the noodles in a separate pan.

- Then at the last minute, add the mushrooms to the meat mixture and cook for 5 minutes.

- Add the sour cream to the meat sauce just before you eat. Serve with the noodles.

HAIR STYLING
PRIVE CLUB
HAIROTIC
CALYPSO
LUX
BAB
Grillroo
General
Robert 1er
Life
MIR*
DÄNKS!

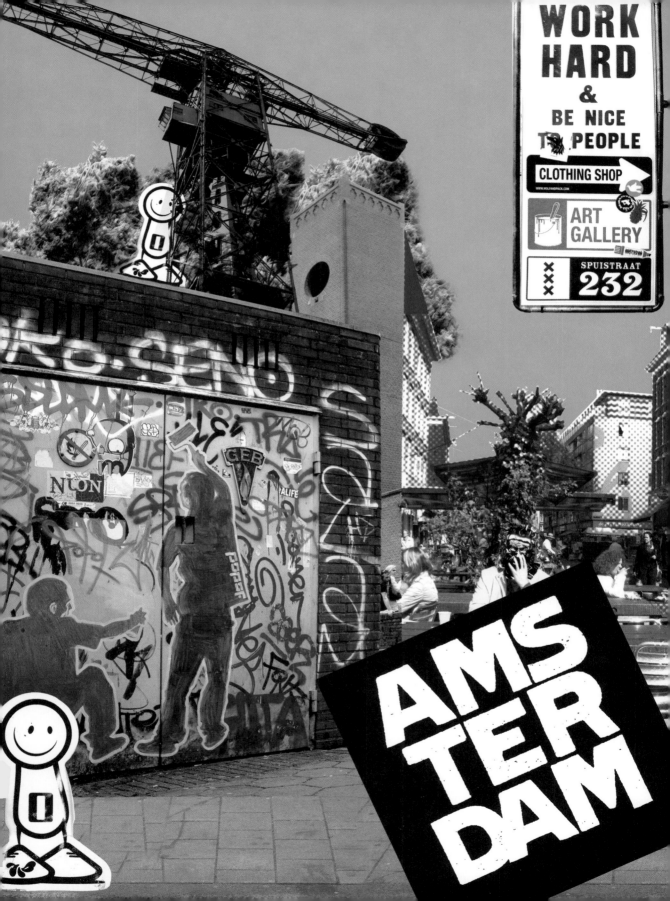

"I'm flying through central Amsterdam; gangs of stags are chanting choruses and staging mock rowdy photo shoots in the narrow alleyways, beers held aloft; the guy taking the photo is shouting 'Look angry, look angry,' and the men growl and snarl, snarl and growl…Click! The photo is taken and…phew! The rest of the street breathes again and the heavy flow of bodies continues along the narrow pavement. The danger has passed. This place is like an XXX-rated Disneyland: full of distractions and sights so strange that you can't help but stare, even though you desperately want to look away….Welcome to the 'Dam."

While preparing to write this chapter I chanced upon the above words, manically scrawled in a notebook I had brought along on my first trip to **Amsterdam** some years ago. Although it's an almost stereotypical, clichéd view of the city, the words sum up a tiny part of the place, a sight that nevertheless must be seen, witnessed and then filed and forgotten. Amsterdam has since become a regular destination of mine. The city is infinitely interesting and is the perfect definition of modern urban culture: the streets are rammed with street art, stencils and stickers, and once you get away from the red light district and coffee shops, the people are so relaxed, polite and cultured that you wonder why every metropolis isn't like this.

Moving in and getting around
I touched down at Schiphol airport. The train ride into the city only took fifteen minutes, as the airport is unusually close to the centre. No need to even think about getting a taxi (that would be a lot slower than the train) – just ask a local. The one thing you'll find lots of in Amsterdam is help. The locals speak great English and often go out of their way to help you find what you're looking for.

Once in the city, I used trains, bikes, motorbikes, buses, boats and trams to get around. The public transport system is one of the best I've ever used. It's lekker – or good, great, cool – as they say in Dutch (and Afrikaans). But the best way by far to move about the city is by bicycle (or a 50 cc motorbike).

The low down
Amsterdam in the 1970s was very tolerant: everything and anything went on sale in the streets, and nobody cared who you were or what you did, or even why you were there. The city attracted some undesirables as a result, but it also appealed to major talent and many bohemians over the years. Not only did Chet Baker die there, but Albert Camus tripped out, Michel van Rijn began his career selling sheepskin coats, and Rutger Hauer met Paul Verhoeven there, who cast him in *Turkish Delight*.

➤ **Transportation Amsterdam style**

European legislation has helped to control the darker side of the city, and ID is required (you have to be over eighteen) if you want to enter the coffee shops (which sell weed or alcohol, but not both). The red light district is marshalled by the Hells Angels, who patrol the streets in groups, keeping rowdy types in check. The Moroccans run the coffee shops (and also control hashish imports) and rival Surinamese and Nigerian gangs fiercely control the street corners for all other drugs. But most of the city's residents don't smoke weed or visit prostitutes: to experience the real Amsterdam you need to forget the coffee shops and red light district. Look through the weed smoke and the red neon haze and you will find…

Cheeky Monday

I spent a few days with the Cheeky Monday family – a group of graffiti and street artists, promoters, DJs and MCs in Amsterdam. I was introduced to the family by DJ Lennox (see p. 184) and these guys helped me out getting around, meeting interesting people, showing me cool shops and telling me where to find the dopest street art.

The Cheeky Monday club happens every Monday night in the Winston Club/Hotel on the Warmoesstraat (see the Hit List). Check out the guy in a gorilla suit who hands out flyers advertising the club beforehand – you can hear the biggest names in drum n bass there for only 6 Euros.

NDSM Werf

For an alternative view of the city, take the ferry (which is free) from behind Centraal Station to NDSM Werf (wharf), one of Amsterdam's lesser know areas of underground culture. There you'll find the Dutch reggae band King Shiloh Sound System (see the Hit List) in an old bunker, the NDSM Hall (a huge venue with a hangar-like structure) and an amazing wall of graffiti in an abandoned dock. MTV have recently moved their headquarters out there too, and while some say this has polluted the once bohemian area with a corporate poison, it suggests that urban youth culture has found a home in this converted wharf. Check out www.ndsm.nl for more details and dates.

De Pijp walk

De Pijp is one of the most ethnically diverse, yet culturally hip, areas in Europe. To visit, take the number 16 or 24 tram south from Centraal Station to Albert Cuypstraat, and then walk east to the Albert Cuypstraat street market. You can't miss it – the street has a market on both sides and you have to walk down the middle between the stalls.

It was in De Pijp that I discovered Turkish pizza (see the recipe on p. 194). There are loads of great places to eat this dish, but I recommend the Orient Doner in the middle of the market on Albert Cuypstraat itself. There are no cars here – people push their bikes instead – so enjoy your food in an area that is full of locals, full of life and full of good vibes. Welcome to De Pijp. When you've finished your Turkish pizza, turn right into Eerste van der Helststraat and check out the pavement cafés. Choose one and chill.

It will take you a while to walk around and discover the neighbourhood for yourself, but you must check out Sarphati Park, where the locals hold birthday parties and picnics at the weekends. To the east of the park you will find Sporadisch Antiquarisch (see the Hit List), a great secondhand art bookshop, which was recommended to me by Erik Kessels (see p. 174). Even when this shop is closed, a selection of books is left outside on the windowsill for you to make your choice (you pay by posting your money through the letterbox). Trust is a great thing.

Another shop worth mentioning is De Emaillekeizer (see the Hit List) in Sweelinckstraat, to the north of the park. This shop sells all things African, loads of reproduction film and music posters and some great reggae records too. And this is one of the only shops in Europe I've ever seen that sells a fantastic range of household items made from recycled cans and tins, including a chest of drawers.

✦ **Graffiti image by the artist 'T' of Anne Frank wearing a Palestinian scarf**

AMSTER DAM 165

Hit List

Shops/galleries

90 Square Meters
Levantplein 52, KNSM Island
(fashion and art)

Ben-G/Patta
Nieuwezijds Voorburgwal 142
(fashion and sneakers)

De Emaillekeizer
1e Sweelinckstraat 15 (gifts)

Hana Zuki
Vijzelstraat 87 (fashion, toys and prints)

Henxs
St Antoniebreestraat 136
(graffiti supply shop)

Rush Hour Records
Spuistraat 98 (tunes and events)

Sporadisch Antiquarisch
Sarphatipark 127 (secondhand art books)

Wolf + Pack
Spuistraat 232 (fashion and art)

Clubs/venues/entertainment

The Winston
Warmoesstraat 131 (club with great hotel
rooms, each decorated by a different artist)

The Melkweg
Lijnbaansgracht 234a
(club and live music venue)

Paradiso
Weteringschans 6–8 (live music venue)

King Shiloh Sound System
NDSM Werf (dub sound system venue
and workshop)

Bioscoop Het Ketelhuis
Pazzanistraat 4 (cinema)

My iPod Playlist

Bubba Sparxxx
Deliverance

Outkast
ATLiens

Underworld
Beaucoup Fish

Brasse Vannie Kaap
BVK

Kwaito
Kwaito Hits

Sigur Rós
()

Lee 'Scratch' Perry
Time Boom X De Devil Dead

Skinnyman
Council Estate of Mind

Clipse
Lord Willin'

Boards of Canada
In a Beautiful Place out in the Country

➔ **A life-size paste-up on the street in Amsterdam**

AMSTERDAM 164

Miss Blackbirdy's World

Miss BLACKBIRDY

Miss Blackbirdy (Merel Boers) is the future of fashion. She is a new breed of designer who mixes street art with *haute couture* in her beautiful, delicately designed creations, all of which feature in her fantasy 'Miss Blackbirdy World'.

Merel only graduated a few years ago but has already won two major fashion awards in the Netherlands: the BLVD Fashion Award 2006 and the Dutch award in the Modern Femininity category during the Amsterdam International Fashion Week in 2007.

My main criticism of urban fashion is that it never progresses beyond the restricted arena of t-shirts and jeans. Miss Blackbirdy's work is the polar opposite of this: her designs are hand-crafted and every detail is custom-made. She lives and works in De Pijp, which provides plenty of inspiration. And although her work is totally fresh, urban and street, there isn't a t-shirt in sight.

www.missblackbirdy.com

King Adz vs Miss Blackbirdy

Nearest city while growing up?
Amsterdam – my grandma lived there.

Who, or what, has had an urban influence in the following areas?
MUSIC: *My motto for everything I make is 'Keep it close to your heart.' There are a lot of people who are doing that in the music that I like at the moment.*
ART: *I like Julie Verhoeven and Piet Paris, head of the Arnhem Modebiënnale. The biennale is a combination of art and fashion, and it makes fashion into an event – something you can believe in: fashion is so much more than just clothes.*
ADVERTISING/MEDIA: *I like those little books you find in bookstores with illustrations and funny stories.*
FASHION: *My fashion friends/old classmates Claire and Jody: the way they live and work is inspiring. I also like Comme des Garçons.*
FILM: *I love Tim Burton's movies – the fantasy of his way of thinking, his colours and the worlds he creates.*
LITERATURE: *I always search for children's books with funny drawings.*
CITY/PLACE: *Amsterdam. I'm so happy when I can ride my bike and there are great places to buy fabrics there too. And I love going to the Noordermarkt on Monday mornings to search for vintage clothing and books.*

How have you made your mark on urban culture?
I make fashion and create illustrations.

What is your favourite food?
My boyfriend Chester's cheese salads.

How to create original fashion
by Miss Blackbirdy

My designs are a combination of fashion and drawing. I might draw a blouse on a piece of paper and then stitch the lines with a sewing machine. Then it's like you can wear a drawing. I make whole collections by bringing 3D lines into 2D drawings.

I created a book containing the Miss Blackbirdy world for my first collection. Using the story of a girl who wants to draw her own dresses, which was the concept of the collection, I wrote and illustrated a story about a bird who came down and helped her make them.

This is the way I always work. I begin with a story. I sketch little figures on white paper. I see a figure and then I create a life around her and her environment: a world in which she lives. This is where I get the inspiration for the print and the design of the collection.

There is always a little bit of emotion in the story. I dream up the story and the lines of text in English, even though it might not be grammatically correct.

I then create a little book made from images and a story and feelings. And then I take something out and make the prints.

Like when a girl spilt some ink on a dress and a bird flew out…

For the Lancôme Colour Design Awards I made up a story about a little girl who looked into her mother's make-up mirror and saw the world of Lancôme. I then made many prints from mirrors and flowers using make-up brushes and mascara.

I try to make new images with things that already exist. The book, the fabric and then the garment. The inspiration for the dress is always that it must be something I'd wear myself. If I would wear it then that is how it should be. Sometimes I let the garment build up over time, adding to it and letting it grow naturally.

When I draw the sketches they are always like the little girl in my Miss Blackbirdy world – light and fragile.

Erik Kessels

Erik is a pioneering creative director and
a founding partner of KesselsKramer
– Holland's most progressive and award-
winning communications and advertising
agency. Erik spends his days creating all forms
of communication: print and TV adverts, books,
branding, events, magazines, kids' TV shows,
newspaper content, guerrilla marketing, film titles,
websites, DVDs and digital content. And as he
does not restrict himself to the world of advertising,
he has a unique perspective on the process and
business of creativity. He is a truly inspiring person,
full of energy and enthusiasm. This is the sort of
guy you want to work for.

One of Erik's many other projects is collecting
random photographs from junk shops, flea markets
and car-boot sales to create content for his
contributions to photography magazines. He also
helped to create the interactive 'Do' brand – which
is ever changing because it asks consumers to add
their own interpretations of products.

www.kesselskramer.nl

ERIK
KESSELS
174

King Adz *vs* **Erik Kessels**

When were your formative years?
After I was born in Roermond, the Netherlands, on 11 March 1966.

Nearest city while growing up?
Eindhoven, the Netherlands.

Who, or what, has had an urban influence in the following areas?
MUSIC: *The Beastie Boys and Motörhead.*
ART: *Andy Warhol.*
DESIGN: *David Carson.*
ADVERTISING/MEDIA: *Tibor Kahlman.*
FASHION: *Jean-Paul Gaultier.*
FILM: Do the Right Thing *(Spike Lee) and* Rumble Fish *(Francis Ford Coppola).*
LITERATURE: *Charles Bukowski and William Burroughs.*
CITY/PLACE: *New York.*

How have you made your mark on urban culture?
Within the field of advertising, KesselsKramer has always tried to break with traditional media: for the Nike campaign we used orange traffic lights and brick walls as a medium, whereas when advertising a budget place to stay in Amsterdam we stuck little flags into Amsterdam's dog shit so as to promote the hotel. To communicate in an urban culture is never the starting point of a project, but it can be the solution to a problem.

What made you realize that urban culture was changing?
Over the last few years I have seen urban culture change rapidly. Young artists cross over with a lot of other disciplines. They became artists, fashion designers, musicians and graphic designers all in one. This happened because these different fields are much easier to access now. An urban artist becomes a medium and a brand.

When was that?
When skateboarder Shepard Fairey stencilled an image of a wrestler called André the Giant at the beginning of the 1990s, he could not have predicted how this image would become a worldwide street icon. This is a great example of how an image can manoeuvre between different disciplines. Nowadays Obey Giant is a skateboard and a poster as well as a fashion brand. This was a change in the modern history of urban culture.

Who should be recognized in this project?
The Dutch designer Helmut Smits (see p. 188) is a big talent at the moment: he crosses over many disciplines and his designs and projects are unlimited.

What is your favourite food?
Frikandel speciaal.

How to get ahead in advertising
by Erik Kessels

The main thing is that you should always work hard and be nice to people. The process I have helped to develop at KesselsKramer goes a little like this. When we start to work for a client or a project, the most important thing is that we talk to the people. It's like when you begin dating someone – you want to make sure that you are going to get on, and so you need a good relationship with the client. This is a crucial part of the process.

We try the clients out and if they like us and we like them, the biggest step is already taken. We don't try to think immediately about media solutions (online, radio, print or TV, etc.) but concentrate more on finding a solution to the problem (usually how to launch a brand or increase sales) and then work out how the message is going to be conveyed. It doesn't matter how the word gets out as long as it is done in the most original way.

We do all this work together with the strategy people – together we try to find a field in which the job can be executed. Then we present the idea. With a large brief we present the strategy first and then the client makes a choice. When that is fixed, we do the creative work. And when that is approved then the production team come in and the idea is executed. So (hopefully) the problem is solved and the client is happy.

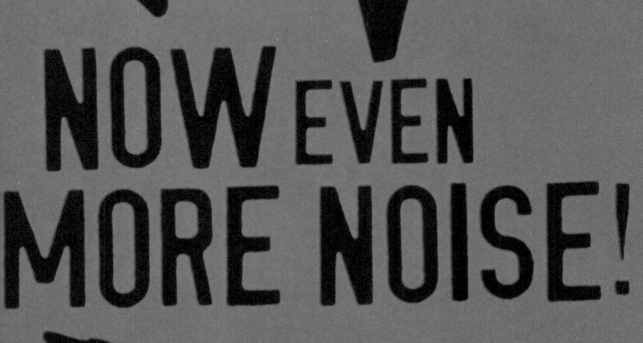

NOW EVEN MORE NOISE!

Hans Brinker
Budget Hotel
Amsterdam
☎ 31 20 6220687

ERIK KESSELS 179

Nina Köll

Nina is a conceptual curator who works with film, art, music and graphics. But to describe her as a curator is a serious understatement: Nina conceptualizes ideas for events, exhibitions, film festivals and then makes them happen. All this adds up to her unique talent as part producer, part director, part artist, part curator and part promoter. She is the ultimate twenty-first century example of modern urban culture in action.

Nina co-founded the Amsterdam Film Experience in 2006 – a festival that blurs the boundaries between film, video and installation art – and she is part of the creative think tank for the LiteSide Festival (a young, multi-disciplinary festival that highlights crossovers between Oriental and European culture). Nina also develops ideas, and curates programmes for TodaysArt, an annual international festival that celebrates modern creativity in the arts. To top it all off, she has just joined the curatorial team of the newly established International Amsterdam Film Festival/MAFIAfest.

www.pepperonina.com

King Adz vs Nina Köll

When were your formative years?
The 1980s – from beginning to end.

Nearest city while growing up?
Innsbruck (small town girl) and Munich (big city lights).

Who, or what, has had an urban influence in the following areas?
MUSIC*: Sun Ra, Herbie Hancock, Lostprophets, DJ Kool Herc, Afrika Bambaataa, Kraftwerk, MC Lyte, NY punk in the 1970s and Mantronix.*
ART*: Jean-Michel Basquiat and graffiti art in general.*
DESIGN*: Stencil aesthetic.*
ADVERTISING/MEDIA*: Music videos, MTV in the 1980s and black vernacular.*
FASHION*: Fashion designers have borrowed from urban fashion rather than influencing it. Generally speaking, I believe that hip hop, punk and electro-funk/electro-hop have influenced street stylez.*
FILM*: Blaxploitation films,* Do the Right Thing *(Spike Lee),* Kids *(Larry Clark),* Colors *(Dennis Hopper),* La Haine *(Mathieu Kassovitz) and* Style Wars *(Tony Silver and Henry Chalfant).*
LITERATURE*: Slam poetry and the spoken word.*
CITY/PLACE*: South Bronx, Brooklyn and Times Square in the late 1970s and 1980s, and Detroit, Brixton (London), Harajuku (Tokyo) and CBGB.*

How have you made your mark on urban culture?
First of all, I moved from an alpine village to London, then to New York and Amsterdam, and ever since I've been actively and creatively participating in urban culture. I live and breathe it.

What made you realize that urban culture was changing?
Through music (on TV).

When was that?
In 1983, as a seven-year-old girl growing up in the Austrian Alps.

Who should be recognized in this project
Kraftwerk and Lostprophet.

What is your favourite food?
Salad, in all possible variations.

NinaKöll
183

DJ Lennox

Lenny has promoted drum n bass ever since it evolved out of jungle and ragga rave. Originally from deepest darkest Essex, he has lived in Amsterdam for the last seven years, and though his involvement in the Cheeky Monday family (see p. 163) has helped build up a drum n bass scene out of nothing.

This is just one of his many talents: Lenny can turn his hand to pretty much anything. He has worked in film, is an accomplished drum n bass and hip hop DJ, and is currently putting the finishing touches to his debut drum n bass album. And after ripping it up on the decks, Lenny gets on the mike too (as MC Lenny Len).

www.myspace.com/lennylenlennox

King Adz vs DJ Lennox

When were your formative years?
I was thirteen when I got my first pair of turntables (Syntronics, belt-driven).

Nearest city while growing up?
London.

Who, or what, has had an urban influence in the following areas?
MUSIC: *Big Daddy Kane, Das EFX and Run-DMC, but I love all kinds of music.*
ART: *Graffiti.*
FASHION: *People who dress themselves and don't do fashion.*
FILM: *Warriors and Wonders.*
LITERATURE: *I've never read a book, but I like comics and porn.*
CITY/PLACE: *Whatever's going on the streets.*

How have you made your mark on urban culture?
Mainly through my career as a DJ, an MC and a promoter. You'll never meet anyone with a bigger passion for drum n bass than me.

What made you realize that urban culture was changing?
When a whole new generation of people started to get into drum n bass. Garage took a lot away from drum n bass back inna day because it was so gangsterish. But the new generation of people who are into their sounds are getting back into drum n bass.

When was that?
Right now.

Who should be recognized in this project?
Shy FX, Mickey Finn, DJ Passion AKA Adam English, DJ Phantasy, DJ Probe and all the Cheeky Monday DJs.

What is your favourite food?
Anything with tomato ketchup.

 **The gorilla mascot for the Cheeky Monday club**

HELMUT SMITS

Helmut Smits

Helmut is a modern artist working in all available media (art, design, sculpture and film) and using all available surfaces (street, advertising hoardings and galleries). His ideas often interact with surrounding communities and environments, and involve customizing standard household objects to give them a new lease of life as objets d'art.

Helmut has exhibited in several countries around the world but doesn't like to travel. One of his most recent projects involved planting a tree in front of an advertising billboard, commenting on visual pollution and bombardment.

He lives in Rotterdam, but exhibits in Amsterdam, and works with KesselsKramer (see p. 174), who have supported his work from the start (which is how all advertising agencies should operate), hence his inclusion in this chapter. Helmut is my favourite Dutch artist, and is slowly but surely building a name for himself in the art world.

www.helmutsmits.nl

★ Helmut Smit's sculpture Paddling
Pool Fountain, 2003
★ Images of the Tree in Front of
Billboard installation from 2006

HELMUT
SMITS

189

King Adz vs *Helmut Smits*

When were your formative years?
From 1997 to 2001.

Nearest city while growing up?
Roosendaal in the Netherlands.

Who, or what, has had an urban influence in the following areas?
MUSIC: *Hip hop in general, not that I'm really happy about that – I like the music not the message.*
ART: *Roman Signer.*
ADVERTISING/MEDIA: *KesselsKramer and TV music channels.*
FASHION: *I'm not really into fashion.*
FILM: *Lars von Trier.*
LITERATURE: *I don't read books.*
CITY/PLACE: *Rotterdam, as far as I am concerned, is the most inspiring city to live in. Shame the air is so bad though.*

How have you made your mark on urban culture?
I just do my thing. I make my sculptures and installations.

Who should be recognized in this project?
Daniel Eatock – I love his way of thinking.

What is your favourite food?
I love all sorts of food, I love going out for dinners: it is the only thing I really spend a lot of money on. Some of my favourite foods include smoked eel, Dutch shrimps, fish in general, most of the dishes my girlfriend prepares and the occasional frikandel speciaal (see the recipe on p. 193).

▶ The inflatable sculpture *Nascar*, 2004, is made of shopping bags, garbage bags, plastic foil and tape

frikandel

Frikandel

This is a dish I first tasted in South Africa. Many Dutch people settled there and maybe on the journey south the ingredients got a bit spiced up. The Dutch like to eat their frikandel (or frikkadel, as they prefer to spell it) as street food. The following version of this spicy hot dog snack food is the best of both worlds…

Feeds 4

Frikandeller
1 **onion, chopped**
3 teaspoons **garlic paste from a jar**
1 tablespoon **sunflower oil (or any cooking oil)**
1 teaspoon **each of fennel seeds, black peppercorns and ground coriander**
2 teaspoons **each of freshly ground nutmeg and ground allspice**
1 tablespoon **curry powder**
500g/1lb 2oz **minced ground beef**
1 **green apple, peeled and grated**
1 **teaspoon salt**
1 **teaspoon Worcestershire sauce**
1 **tablespoon white vinegar**
a handful of **fresh coriander, chopped**

Garlic mashed potatoes
500g/1lb 2oz **potatoes**
20ml/7fl oz **milk**
a tablespoon of **butter**
2 teaspoons **garlic paste from a jar**
salt and black pepper

Sauce
1 **onion, sliced**
1 tablespoon **sunflower oil**
1 teaspoon **curry powder**
1 tablespoon **plain flour**
250ml/9fl oz **milk, warmed**
1 tablespoon **white vinegar**
2 tablespoons **mango chutney**

- For the frikandeller, fry the onion and garlic paste in the oil until transparent. Add all the spices and continue frying for 2 minutes. Remove from the heat and allow to cool.

- Then add the beef and the remaining ingredients. Mix thoroughly before taking little bits of the mixture and making into 12 balls (Afrikaans-style) or sausages (Dutch-style). Press the balls flat to form a disk shape (or leave as a sausage). Fry, grill or BBQ for 10–15 minutes, until thoroughly cooked.

- While the frikandeller are cooking, peel and chop the potatoes in half, boil until cooked and drain.

- Mash the potatoes with milk, butter and garlic paste, and season to taste.

- For the sauce, fry the onion in the oil until transparent. Add the curry powder and flour, mix well and cook for 5 minutes. Add the heated milk, vinegar and chutney, and simmer for another 5 minutes.

- Serve the frikandeller on top of the garlic mashed potatoes and pour over the sauce.

FRIKANDEL
193

Lahmacun

I discovered this Turkish recipe while wandering around the De Pijp area of Amsterdam. It looks a bit like a normal pizza but when you eat it you'll taste the difference. It's a good TV snack. And I have included a traditional pizza option for added value!

Feeds 2–4

Pizza base

300g/2½ cups **plain flour, sifted**
5g/1¼ teaspoons **dry yeast**
1 teaspoon **salt**
175ml/6fl oz/¾ cup **warm water**
1 tablespoon **milk**
2 teaspoons **olive oil**

Topping

250g/9oz **minced meat (lamb or beef, or a mixture)**
1 small jar **salsa**
2 teaspoons **garlic paste from a jar**

To serve

lemon juice
mayonnaise
salad made with lettuce, cucumber and tomato
chopped chillies

- To make the base, place all the ingredients in a bowl, except for the olive oil, and mix for 5 minutes until a smooth dough is formed. If the mixture is too wet then just add a little more flour. The final consistency should be soft but not wet. Place the dough in an olive-oil-smeared bowl, cover it with a damp tea-towel, place somewhere warm and allow to rise for an hour or so.

- After the dough has doubled in size, grease a baking tray and roll out the dough into two bases the size of a large dinner plate.

- Mix all the topping ingredients together and spread over the dough. Bake in a preheated oven at 190°C/375°F/Gas 5 for 20 minutes.

- Remove from the oven, sprinkle with lemon juice and whack on some mayonnaise, salad and chopped chillies. Roll into a wrap-sized snack and eat in front of the telly…

- For a traditional pizza, just replace the above toppings with grated mozzarella and cheddar, a small jar salsa and any combination of the following: sliced meat (salami, pepperoni, smoked ham), chopped mushrooms or peppers, olives and anchovies.

I-tal vegetable stew

Easy now star! I-tal is a Rasta/Jamaican term for food without salt, and this recipe is in honour of the King Shiloh Sound System who gave me a tasty tour of their NDSM headquarters. Jah Rastafari!

Feeds 4–6

3 **cloves garlic**
2 teaspoons **fresh thyme**
2 **large potatoes**
1 **large plantain**
2 **sweet potatoes**
3 **medium carrots**
12 **medium okras (frozen is cool)**
1 can **kidney bean or chickpeas, drained**
900ml/2 pints/5 cups **vegetable stock**
3 **spring onions, chopped**
1 **scotch bonnet chilli pepper, chopped**
2 teaspoons **ground allspice**
black pepper
2 **large tomatoes, chopped**
200g/7oz **canned sweetcorn, drained**
400ml/14oz **coconut milk**
55g/2oz **self-raising flour**
55g/2oz **beef suet (lard)**
a tablespoon of **butter**
a handful of **fresh coriander, chopped**

- Chop the garlic and thyme together. Peel and chop the potatoes, plantain, sweet potatoes, carrots and okra.

- In a large pan, put the kidney beans on to boil in the stock with the spring onions, scotch bonnet pepper, thyme and garlic mixture, allspice and some black pepper. Cook for 10 minutes, then add the chopped vegetables, the tomato and sweetcorn and cook for a further 20 minutes. Then add the coconut milk and return to a low heat.

- Meanwhile, mix the flour and suet with a little water to make small dumplings (spinners). Then add these to the pot, cover and cook on a low heat for 25 minutes.

- Add the butter, garnish with coriander and serve immediately.

Veggie pasta

There is a wicked selection of alternative/organic street food options in Amsterdam. This is one dish I've been cooking for years that would go down well on the menu of any veggie restaurant.

Feeds 4

1 tablespoon **cooking oil**
1 **onion, chopped**
3 **courgettes (zucchini), sliced**
1 bunch **broccoli, separated into small florets**
salt and black pepper
1 **red pepper, chopped into small pieces the width of a finger**
1 **orange pepper, chopped into small pieces the width of a finger**
chilli sauce
2 tablespoons **soy sauce**
450g/1lb **spaghetti (or other pasta)**
freshly grated Parmesan

- Heat the oil and fry the onion until golden. Add the courgettes and fry gently for about 5 minutes.

- In another pan, parboil the broccoli in salted water for about 5 minutes.

- Add the chopped peppers to the onion and courgette mixture. Drain the broccoli (but remember to save the water), and add it, with chilli sauce to taste (optional), soy sauce and black pepper, to the pan of vegetables. Cook on a very low heat while you cook the pasta.

- Boil the spaghetti or your favourite type of pasta in boiling salted water (or, better, the broccoli water for extra flavour) until al dente.

- Drain the spaghetti and add to the vegetable pan, mix thoroughly with the vegetables, add some more soy sauce (or more chilli sauce if you prefer), and serve topped with grated Parmesan.

Mince curry and peas

*This is a lekker Cape Malay recipe brought home (a reverse of the Frikandel's journey)
by the Dutch returning to Holland on holiday from Cape Town.*

Feeds 4

2 teaspoons **vegetable oil**
1 large **onion, sliced**
1 can **tomatoes**
3 pieces **cinnamon bark**
5 **cardamom pods**
3 **cloves**
3 teaspoons **garam masala**
1 teaspoon **turmeric**
4 teaspoons **ground cumin**
1 teaspoon **ground coriander**
1 teaspoon **ginger paste from a jar**
3 teaspoons **garlic paste from a jar**
500g/1lb 2oz **minced ground steak
  or lamb**
425ml/¾ pint/scant 2 cups **stock
  (the same as your meat of choice)**
4 **potatoes, peeled and quartered**
200g/7oz **frozen peas**

• Heat the oil in a large pan, add the onion and fry until
  golden. Add the can of tomatoes and cook on a low heat
  for 10 minutes. Then add all the spices and simmer for
  about 15 minutes, stirring frequently.

• Add the mince, allow to brown, and then add the stock
  and cook for at least 30 minutes on the lowest heat,
  stirring constantly.

• Add the potatoes to the mixture and cook for another
  15 minutes, or until the potatoes begin to crumble,
  adding more stock if needed – you want it to be fairly
  wet. Finally, add the frozen peas and cook for 5 minutes.

• Serve with Indian breads such as rotis or parathas.

Spinach and goat's cheese pasta

This is a good example of how street food has developed into one of the most popular of foods. When I was a youth, most cafés only sold badly fried food, but these days this dish is more likely to be served, and wouldn't seem out of place, in any decent bar or café with street art on the walls.

Feeds 4

6 **large tomatoes**
3 **cloves garlic, chopped**
2 **chillies (red and green)**
1 tablespoon **olive oil**
500g/18oz **conchiglie pasta**
salt and black pepper
300g/11oz **spinach**
300g/11oz **soft round goat's cheese, chopped**

- Chop the tomatoes into quarters, place on an ovenproof tray and cook in the oven at 200°C/400°F/Gas 6 for 20 minutes.

- Chop the garlic and chillies and fry in the oil for about 5 minutes until browned.

- Cook the pasta (check the pack for times) in a large pan of salted boiling water.

- Wash and place the spinach in a colander and then drain the pasta (when cooked) over the top of the spinach (thereby part cooking it).

- Put the spinach and pasta back into the pan and add the garlic, chillies, tomatoes and chopped goat's cheese.

- Cook on a low heat until the cheese has melted. Season to taste with black pepper.

אואו ✡
Grillroom

Pepers
€ 1,40
Per 100 Gram

FRUITVEILING 1980

MARGRATEN

Peri-peri chicken and spicy rice

What goes around comes around, and this is another colony-inspired recipe that has made it into the mainstream. Peri-peri is an African and Portuguese term for small birds-eye chillies. So, from Portugal to Africa to Holland. The real urban cooking experience: picking up influences on the road…

Feeds 4–6

5 teaspoons **each of garlic and ginger pastes from a jar**
2 **chilli peppers, chopped**
a large squirt **of tomato ketchup or sweet chilli sauce (your choice)**
25ml/1fl oz **lemon juice**
2 teaspoons **peri-peri spice blend**
a bunch of **fresh coriander, chopped**
1kg/2¼lb **chicken pieces, washed and scored with a sharp knife**

Spicy rice

400g/14oz **basmati rice**
1 **chicken stock cube dissolved in**
425ml/¾ pint/scant 2 cups **water**
1 **onion, finely chopped**
2 teaspoons **peri-peri spice blend**
1 **green and** 1 **red pepper, finely chopped**

- In a large bowl mix the garlic and ginger pastes with the chilli, ketchup, lemon juice, peri-peri spice blend and chopped coriander. Add the chicken pieces one by one, making sure they are thoroughly coated with the spice mixture. Leave to marinate for at least an hour (overnight is best).

- To cook, either roast in the oven at 190°C/375°F/Gas 5 for 60 minutes or BBQ (by far the best way).

- Meanwhile, wash and soak the rice for 30 minutes in a large pan. Drain, then add the chicken stock, onion, peri-peri spice blend and peppers. Cover the rice pan and when boiling, turn down to the lowest setting and cook for 20 minutes.

- Serve the chicken with the spicy rice.

PERI-PERI
CHICKEN
205

Potjiekos

This is a classic dish. A potjiekos is the pot used to cook the dish in (it looks a bit like a mini witch's cauldron).

Feeds 6–8

2 teaspoons **paprika**
25g/1oz **plain flour**
500g/1lb 2oz **beef stewing steak, cubed**
1 tablespoon **cooking oil**
a tablespoon **of butter**
2 **onions, chopped**
100g/²/₃ cup **barley**
5 **carrots, peeled and sliced**
2 **leeks, sliced**
2 teaspoons **garlic paste from a jar**
3 teaspoons **mixed dried herbs**
300ml/½ pint/1¼ cups **beer or wine**
425ml/¾ pint/scant 2 cups **beef stock**
1 packet **tomato soup powder**
1 **bay leaf**
1 tablespoon **white vinegar**
2 tablespoons **cornflour**
salt and black pepper

- Combine the paprika and the flour in a bowl and add the meat cubes, lightly coating the meat in the mixture. In a large pan, brown the meat in the oil and butter for about 5 minutes. Remove the meat from the pan and set aside.

- In the same pan, fry the onion until tender and then add the barley, carrots, leeks and garlic and simmer for 5 minutes.

- Return the meat to the pan and stir in the herbs, beer, stock, soup powder and bay leaf. Replace the lid and simmer until the meat is tender, for at least 1 hour. Cook for as long as possible, adding water and stirring every 20 minutes.

- Finally, mix the vinegar and cornflour and stir into the potjiekos. Simmer until the gravy has thickened, then season with salt and pepper.

- Serve with veg of your choice. It also goes well with French fries and peas…

"I grew up in the 1970s on the outskirts of London, just where the grey starts to turn green. My earliest memory of the city is going to Kentucky Fried Chicken opposite King's Cross station and how dope I thought it was when I got my first can of Pepsi, some tepid chips and a greasy bit of chicken. The food was shite, but that's beside the point: it was the urban experience of eating food on the street (and on the train) that will stay with me forever."

The Mud Club

My first multi-cultural urban experience was at the Mud Club – the Friday nightclub hosted by Philip Salon in Busby's on Charing Cross Road. DJs Jay Strongman, Mark Moore and Tasty Tim would drop hip hop there, and it was out of this scene that Acid House developed. Although it began in Ibiza, Acid House became an element of English youth culture that had an effect on many levels of society. This was my rite of passage into urban culture and I was lucky to be living **London** and studying in when it was all happening.

Street level

One of the main contributions to urban culture to come out of London is the limited edition street art print, offering anyone with a few hundred quid the chance to own a signed piece of street art history. So popular is this recent phenomenon that when Banksy releases a print (via www.picturesonwalls. com) the server melts with the number of people trying to get hold of his prints.

Many more counter- and sub-cultures have crossed over from the streets of London into mainstream global consciousness (punks, for example), although none as important as today's street art:

Banksy blew up on London streets, Invader (see p. 92) recently put up his one hundredth mosaic invader there and Jimmy Cauty (ex-KLF) now pastes his art in the city. The West End is full of stickers (quicker to apply) and the City of London, from Old Street to Whitechapel via Hoxton, boasts graffiti, stencils and posters. And this is where you'll find the coolest shops, galleries, cafes and restaurants, bars and venues. This is London's East Village and Lower East Side.

Street art walk

My guide to the ultimate in urban art in London was the street artist Pure Evil, who knows his stuff better than anyone. Here is one of the many walks we have made around Brick Lane, Shoreditch and London Fields. Start by getting off the tube at Aldgate East and walking east along Whitechapel Road. Turn left into Osborn Street and keep walking up as it turns into Brick Lane, checking out all the sights until you reach the Truman Brewery (see the Hit List). When you've had your fill, keep walking north along Brick Lane until you reach Sclater Street on your left and follow this until it turns into Bethnal Green Road. If you keep walking in the same direction you will reach Shoreditch High Street: turn right onto this busy road and walk north until you get to Bateman's Row. If you turn left onto this street you will see a Banksy piece as

◆ **'Wall of Fame' on Brick Lane in the East End of London**

LONDON 209

you walk along. And at the end of the street, when you turn right onto Curtain Road, look for the work by Invader. At the end of this road, turn left onto Rivington Street and left again onto Ravey Street, continuing until you reach Blackall Street. Turn right here and walk up to the end before turning left onto Paul Street and then right into Leonard Street. Check out the street art on the big blue circle in the middle of the street and then continue walking up to City Road. At the end of this road, turn right and shortly you will find Old Street tube station in front of you. This walk should take you about half a day if you check out everything on the way. See the Hit List for other places to visit en route.

Street food
London's multi-culturalism means one thing: wicked Chinese, Jamaican, Indian, Thai and Vietnamese food. The very nature of street food, like street art, can mean that it is here today and gone tomorrow. But luckily the areas where it is available in London are pretty much the same, year in, year out. Ladbroke Grove, Brixton and Balham are good places to eat Jamaican food and you'll find some serious Jerk Chicken at the Dalston end of Kingsland Road. Stoke Newington has the best Turkish and Kurdish restaurants, and I always visit Testi (see the Hit List) when I'm hanging out at Jonathan Olley's yard (see p. 226), which is only a few minutes' walk away.

The Low down
London, along with New York, has played an important part in the development of urban street culture, and street art has often had a direct influence on the areas in which it appears. Old Street, Hoxton and Shoreditch were influential areas a decade ago and are still great places to be. But when an arty/creative crowd move into a run-down area and make it a desirable and trendy place to live, property prices go up. The cool arty crowd then have to begin again somewhere else – in London's case, in neighbourhoods like Victoria Park, London Fields and Bethnal Green. These are the places to watch over the next few years.

♦ **Street art on Leonard Street near City Road in London**

Hit List

Galleries

Black Rat Press Gallery
  Arch 461, 83 Rivington Street

Lazarides Gallery
  8 Greek Street

Pure Evil Gallery
  108 Leonard Street

The Spitz
  109 Commercial Street, Old Spitalfields Market

StolenSpace Gallery
  Dray Walk, The Old Truman Brewery,
  91 Brick Lane

Bars

The Dragon Bar
  Shoreditch High Street

Dream Bags Jaguar Shoes
  34–36 Kingsland Road

Shopping

Daddy Kool Records
  12 Berwick Street

Dub Vendor Record Shack
  150 Ladbroke Grove

No-one Fashion
  1 Kingsland Road

Grand OFR Bookshop
  The Old Truman Brewery, 91 Brick Lane

Playlounge
  19 Beak Street (games and gadgets)

Record and Tape Exchange
  229 Camden High Street

Zwemmer Books
  80 Charing Cross Road

Food

Irie Jamaican Café
  172 New Cross Road

Super Star
  17 Lisle Street
  (best Dim Sum in London)

Take Two
  1 Brixton Station Road
  (Great JA patties)

Testi
  38 Stoke Newington High Street

My iPod Playlist

The Streets
  Original Pirate Material

Eternal
  'I Belong in You' (White Label)

Coco
  'Sunday Morning' (White Label)

A Guy Called Gerald
  'Voodoo Ray'

KLF
  Space

Skinnyman
  Council Estate of Mind

Smashing Pumpkins
  Adore

Brian Eno and David Byrne
  My Life in the Bush of Ghosts

◄ **Jack the Ripper armed with
a spray can in an alley near
Brick Lane, London**

FOR
SKATE

DOWNEY

Leigh Bowery

INSERT YOUR
LIFE STORY
HERE

OXIC
IENDS

BINA SHOES

LONDON
215

bigshinything.com
Anne-Fay Townsend

Bigshinything.com focuses on all things cultural, including modern philosophy, and is run by Anne-Fay in her spare time. The main emphasis of the website is to showcase the progressive use of technology in art, media and culture, but it also looks at the unusual and the irrelevant, as well as emerging media. It is one of the few websites that I make sure to check every day.

www.bigshinything.com

➧ **A collapsed building on Commercial Road, London, photographed by Darrell Berry**

e. ail: o@cityt x.co.uk

I T ⊃ (2 7 7

BUSI ESS AS USU L → →

King Adz vs *Anne-Fay Townsend*

When were your formative years?
I was a teenager in the 1980s. I got stuck between post-punk and rave, missing one and avoiding the other.

Nearest city while growing up?
Birmingham.

Who, or what, has had an urban influence in the following areas?
MUSIC: *There's no one musician that I can name – there are so many. But there are also loads that like to claim an urban influence when there is none: Lily Allen comes to mind. Music-on-demand services like iTunes and Napster are completely changing people's relationship with music in a positive way: nothing is too niche any more and taste isn't prescribed by those who are selling the most records. This is excellent for some types of music that wouldn't get exposure outside of clubs or pirate radio.*
ART: *It's odd to me that people think that the current merging of urban and high art (like Banksy selling at auction) is anything new. Keith Haring and Jean-Michel Basquiat were doing exactly the same thing in the 1980s and their art still resonates today. I think that an artist like Wolfgang Tillmans does a lot to represent his particular bit of urban culture in a truthful but visually stunning way. His photos of gay clubs always make me cry.*
DESIGN: *Thomas Heatherwick has done a lot to make public sculpture relevant, especially his recent installation at Guy's Hospital in*

London. Even Antony Gormley has been important, although I think he's not as much fun as Heatherwick: Heatherwick's stuff is fantastically bonkers. Someone like Philippe Starck is also important, just because his influence seems to be everywhere now, especially in the bar and club scene. Personally, I'd like to see someone else given a go.
ADVERTISING/MEDIA: *HHCL's advertising for Tango in the 1990s showed how advertising could enter the vernacular. Being 'Tango'ed' is still in use as a phrase in playgrounds and in the media today, a good ten years after the campaign broke. (Full disclosure: I worked for HHCL from 1997 to 2005.) That said, I think advertising is pretty much over as a medium: it's too easy to avoid nowadays and I think kids just tune it out. The self-made media of blogs and YouTube are much more important and influential: just look at the individual designs of most MySpace pages. Blogs such as DListed and Go Fug Yourself started as hobbies but are now mini-media empires. They are creating their own language as well as reporting what's on the street in a way that the mainstream media can never do.*
FASHION: *John Galliano and Alexander McQueen are probably the two designers who have the most 'trickle-down' influence in the UK. During the punk era Vivienne Westwood showed how the barriers can become blurred between high fashion and street fashion, and we're starting to*

see a similar movement with designers like Gareth Pugh who are aligned to the club scene. Also coming from the clubs, streetwear designers like Cassette Playa are forcing trends such as New Rave into the mainstream.

FILM: *This is probably an age thing, but I think* Trainspotting *was the first film to portray clubbing in way that didn't make me cringe.* 24 Hour Party People *had a pretty good go as well. For a film that really gets under the skin of a sub-culture,* Paris is Burning *is still amazing.*

LITERATURE*: Writers like James Kelman and Irvine Welsh have done an amazing job in writing books that read like real people wrote them. When Kelman won the Booker Prize for* How Late It Was, How Late *there was an outcry because it was written in the Scots vernacular. That kind of snobbery doesn't happen any more.*

CITY/PLACE*: London, obviously, is a hub. But then I don't travel enough.*

How have you made your mark on urban culture?
I write a blog called bigshinything.com that comments on street and emergent art, and other stuff that interests me.

What made you realize that urban culture was changing?
I don't think that culture has changed per se – youth culture is always going to mutate and grow. But the tools with which artists and kids can now share culture with each other have had an enormous effect. Look at the explosion in street art blogs such as Wooster and Hacktivism: these would have been niche activities with limited channels for expression prior to the existence of the internet. Any period of political instability and the oppression of freedoms brings with it an explosion of creative expression too: the Wooster Collective (see p. 44) came out of the proliferation of street art in New York post-9/11 and the invasion of Afghanistan.

When was that?
I guess the current explosion in tech and online stuff started to happen around 2001. Again, the current political situation has also given things an almighty shove: people have got something to push against.

Who should be recognized in this project?
I think that Regine over at the blog We-Make-Money-not-Art.com does an amazing job in cataloguing new art and new tech products. And the guys at Wooster Collective.

bigshinything
.com
221

D*Face

D*Face is one of the most prolific street artists of his generation and he is definitely *the* London street artist to watch. Using a family of dysfunctional characters who send a jolt of subversion through today's media-saturated environment, he works with a variety of media and techniques. D*Face wants us not just to 'see' but to 'look' at the increasingly bizarre popular culture that surrounds our lives.

Over the past eight years, D*Face has exhibited across the world, and also opened the Outside Institute – the first ever gallery devoted to street art in London. D*Face now runs the gallery StolenSpace (see Hit List) in Brick Lane, which is both a stage for his latest work, and a launch pad for new artists.

www.dface.co.uk

▸ -17 Degrees, 2006, an ice sculpture by D*Face located in the Arctic Circle

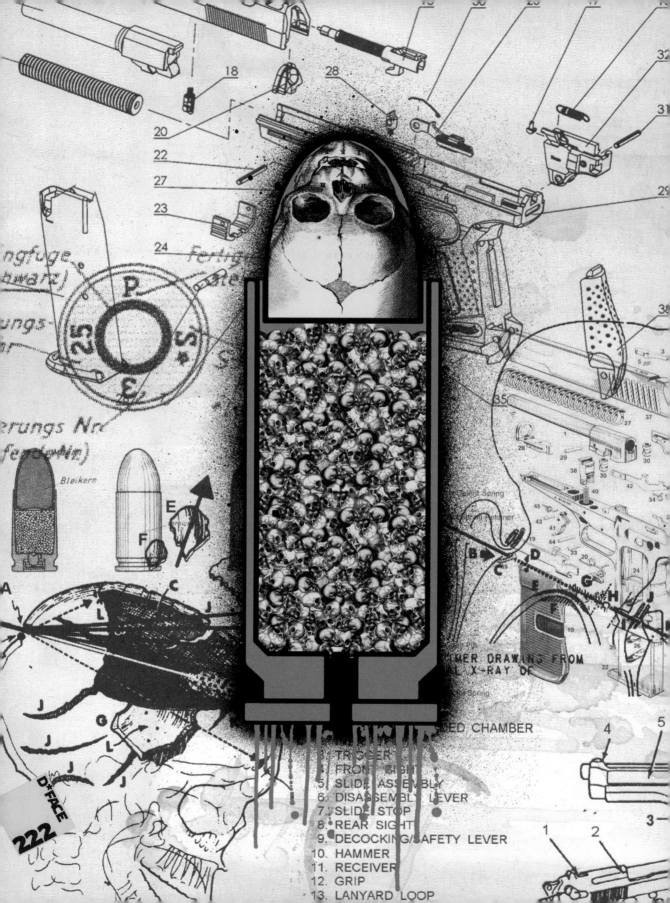

King Adz vs D*Face

When were your formative years?
Umm, not sure. Ask my mum.

Nearest city while growing up?
London.

Who, or what, has had an urban influence in the following areas?
MUSIC: *Sex Pistols.*
ART: *Pop Art and graffiti writers such as Cost and Revs.*
DESIGN: *None.*
ADVERTISING/MEDIA: *None.*
FASHION: *None.*
FILM: *Style Wars.*
LITERATURE: *Spray Can Art.*
CITY/PLACE: *New York and Barcelona.*

How have you made your mark on urban culture?
For the past year my work has been focused on money and fame. As Wu-Tang Clan versed in their album Enter the Wu-Tang (36 Chambers), *'Cash rules everything around me.' This statement still rings true as we witness the paths of destruction our leaders pursue in order to fuel our ever increasing appetite for a material, voyeuristic, disposable, buy-now-pay-later, put-it-on-plastic life.*

What made you realize that urban culture was changing?
I guess the most obvious sign was that while skateboarding my teen years away I was seen as an outcast or an outsider, and the things I liked were frowned upon by the mainstream. But look at skateboarding now: there are schools that specialize in teaching it and it's the biggest growth sports industry.

When was that?
I guess it must have been fifteen years ago.

Who should be recognized in this project?
The unknown and forgotten writers who painted the track sides that I passed daily as a kid. Those people had a huge influence on me and on my work.

✦ **Artwork for a screen print of** *Guns are for Idiots* **by D*Face**

The art of D.I.Y.
by D*Face

All I really wanted to do was skate and doodle. Even when I was studying for a design and illustration degree I was always doing my own stuff outside the course. When I got an illustration and design job I was immediately frustrated. It was meant to be creative, but it wasn't what I'd spent the last five years building up to do.

So I spent all my free time using the vast facilities that these agencies offered – like unlimited photocopying and art supplies. For free. And because I was bored, and it was a bit of fun, I would paste up my work on the way home. But this was in 1998 or 1999, before anything was labelled 'street art'.

I mainly worked on stickers at first because there was another guy in the office who I'd work and doodle with, and he was into the same stuff as me. At the end of the day we'd screw up the piles of doodled paper, but I figured that if I started drawing them on vinyl I could stick them up in the street.

The first characters were called INSTANT and were like buttons and toggles and switches

– it was about having everything at the press of a button. I felt disheartened with the material nature of the creative industry so perhaps these stickers were a reaction to the work I was doing at the agency. I drew up a character that would fit symmetrically into the shape of a six-foot bus box marked on the road by a bus stop and the D*Face square head character was born, just because it fitted in there nicely.

I chose the bus boxes as my canvas, my billboard, because they were really visible. I wanted to link the routes I took through the city, so instead of getting a bus from work to the station or to the pub I'd walk, and hit as many boxes as I could on the way. And the next time I went that way I would try and fill in and finish off the route, or I'd take a different route and try to link the boxes up. In time they became visual reminders of where I'd been across London. It was as simple as that. I didn't know that anyone was paying attention to my work, and I didn't care because it was just idle, self-indulgent fun.

*▶ **Drone Dog** sculpture by D*Face and Ben Johnson, located outside StolenSpace gallery in London*

Jonathan Olley

Jonathan Olley is a London-based photographer
who has documented the transformation of
Eastern Europe, including the fall of the Berlin Wall
and the wars in former Yugoslavia. He attended
Chelsea School of Art with the intention of studying
fine art, but after discovering the war photography of
Don McCullin and Lee Miller, Jonathan determined
that photography was the best way to combine his
artistic and social interests.

Winner of the World Press Photo, the Observer
Hodge Award and Young Photojournalist of the Year
in 1995, Jonathan is an accomplished international
documentary photographer who has captured the
fury and the beauty of Europe's war zones, and
the complex social developments of urban centres
around the world.

His work has been exhibited in The Photographers'
Gallery, the ICA and Tate Britain in London, and he
has taken part in the Photofestival Groningen in the
Netherlands and Visa pour l'Image – the international
photojournalism festival in Perpignan, France,
among others.

www.jonathanolley.com

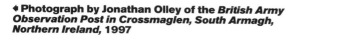

✦ **Photograph by Jonathan Olley of the *British Army
Observation Post in Crossmaglen, South Armagh,
Northern Ireland*, 1997**

King Adz vs **Jonathan Olley**

When were your formative years?
From 1979 to 1989.

Nearest city while growing up?
London.

Who, or what, has had an urban influence in the following areas?
MUSIC: *Happy Mondays, 808 State, The Inspiral Carpets, Oasis (sadly), LA-inspired hip hop 'culture', Nirvana, Korn, Limp Bizkit and Linkin Park.*
ART: *Tagging and Banksy.*
DESIGN: *Manga, deconstruction and disposable culture.*

ADVERTISING/MEDIA: *Tango (the 'You've been Tango'ed' ads), the rise of the Yankee 4x4, yoof/lad culture, the ladette, WAIF and WAG culture, digital photography and camera phones.*
FASHION: *The rise of the celebrity, showing off yer wad and thus the rise of big (read expensive) names like D&G, Versace, Tiffany and Lexus, etc.*
FILM: *Tarantino (sadly), the gangster genre, Vin Diesel-type films and home-made celeb porn (in the style of Paris Hilton and Pamela Anderson).*

▼ *Daintree Rainforest, Cairns, Queensland, Australia, 2006* ◆ *Flood at Glastonbury Festival, 2005*

LITERATURE: *Do people read anything other than* Hello!, OK!, Heat, Closer, *Harry fuckin' Potter and online instructions about how to make a pipe bomb?*
CITY/PLACE: *Los Angeles.*

How have you made your mark on urban culture?
I got married and had children.

What made you realize that urban culture was changing?
When some kids called me a mad old fucker, and when I threw stones back at them.

When was that?
Yesterday.

Who should be recognized in this project?
Jade Goody. She has single-handedly made stupidity and ignorance acceptable. Awwww. Donchajusluvver! And Victoria Beckham for conjoining bad taste, excess, lack of talent and stupidity and then making gazillions.

What is your favourite food?
Brown crab-meat sandwiches.

How to take a pukka photo

by Jonathan Olley

Taking a good picture can be reduced to a single element: **WHERE YOU STAND WHEN YOU TAKE THE PICTURE**. In its raw essence, this is all you need to know about how to take a picture. The technical stuff you can learn from a book and the rest is the application of experience. Oh! And it helps to marry an understanding partner, to follow your own path, to work to your own agenda and not to be distracted, beautiful people, offspring and large bundles of cash aside.

◆ *EOD (Explosive Ordinance Disposal), Yugoslav-made 180mm Mortar Bomb, South Eastern Iraq, 2004*

Skinnyman

Skinnyman is the UK's finest, and most notorious, MC: his killer debut album *Council Estate of Mind* (see the Hit List) has been steadily selling for a couple of years and he has a reputation for being as real as his lyrics. I hooked up with him at his hotel in Newcastle, an hour before he is about to perform and a few hours before I'm due to fly to Berlin, so we don't have time in abundance.

After about ten minutes in his room, there's a tapping at the door and a hotel minion asks us to keep the noise down because there have been some complaints. But we weren't making any noise: we'd been talking about art (Andy Warhol, Banksy and Keith Haring) and music (Nas, Baby J and Lupe Fiasco).

Skinny is not feeling it tonight. He takes a shower and then there's more banging on the door. The duty manger storms in and starts yelling at us about making too much noise. Skinny holds back for as long as he can but it's obvious that the hotel is looking for an excuse to throw us out. 'We're leaving your shitty hotel,' Skinny tells him. The duty manager minces out. Skinny packs and we wait by the lift. But when the doors opens, six police officers and the hotel manager burst out like storm troopers. 'That's him! That's him!' the manager points at Skinny. And this is when it kicks off.

A short time into the madness somebody points out that I am in fact an impartial witness, and a member of the media. Everything calms down once the hotel and police realize this might be written about.

I bundle Skinny into the lift and we depart. He doesn't play the show (I don't blame him) and I have to rush to catch my flight.

www.myspace.com/mcskinnyman

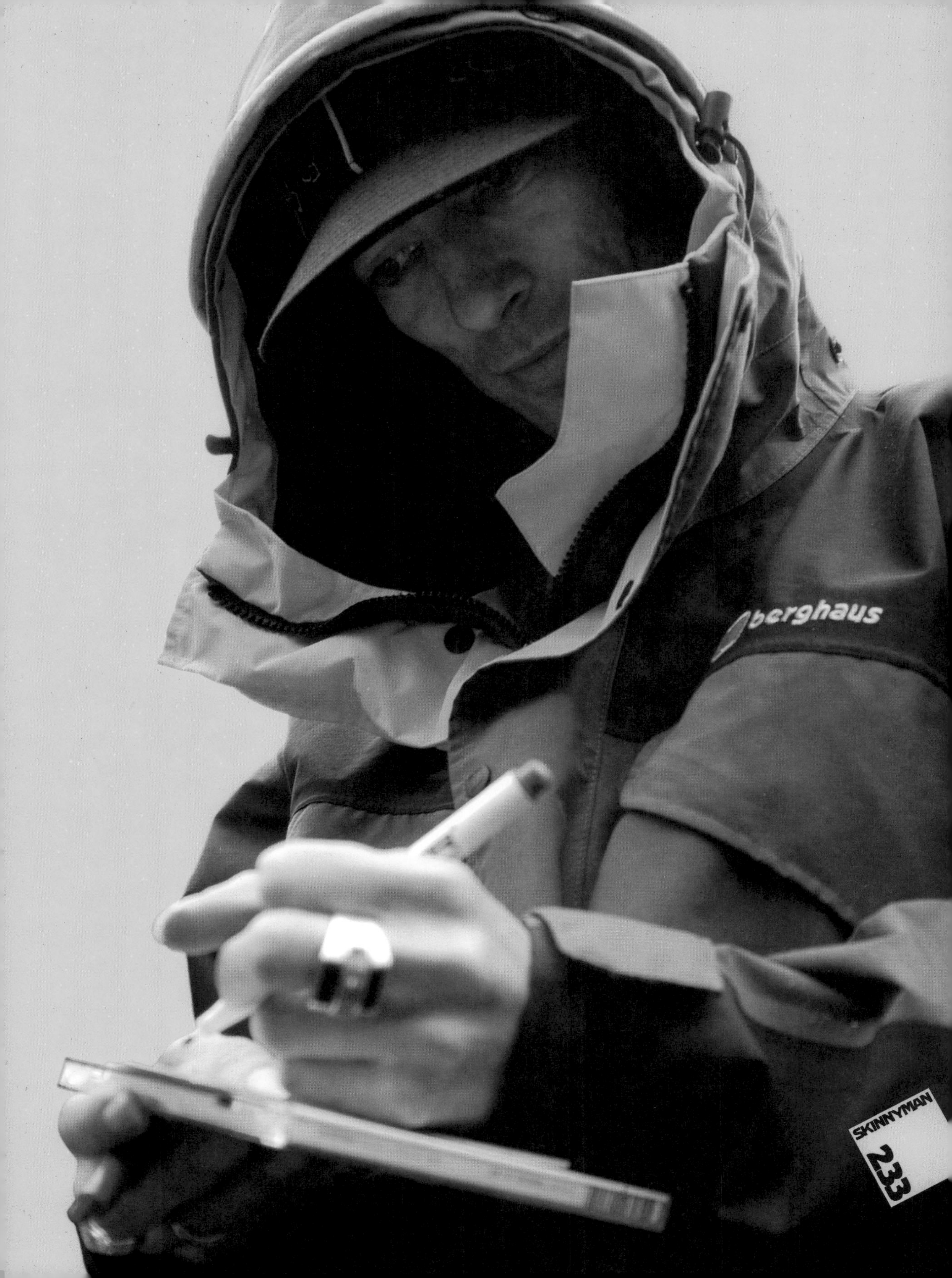
berghaus
SKINNYMAN
233

King Adz vs **Skinnyman**

When were your formative years?
From 1979 to 1984.

Nearest city while growing up?
Leeds, and then London.

Who, or what, has had an urban influence in the following areas?
MUSIC*: Bob Marley, Gil Scott-Heron, The Last Poets, Poor Righteous Teachers, KRS-ONE, Dead Prez, Capelton and Sizzla/ Comanche.*
ART*: Robo484 (WRH Crew) and Vaughn and Barbara Bode.*
DESIGN*: The BMX.*
ADVERTISING/MEDIA*: R. White's Lemonade.*
FASHION*: Jean-Paul Gaultier and Marc Buchanan/Pelle Pelle.*
FILM*: Bugsy Malone, Planet of the Apes and Bowling for Columbine.*
LITERATURE*: George Orwell and Chancellor Williams.*
CITY/PLACE*: Bristol.*

How have you made your mark on urban culture?
I brought forth the voice of the frustrated inner city/urban youth.

What made you realize that urban culture was changing?
Music is created to elevate the listener; therefore we will forever have change.

When was that?
In mass culture, music repeats itself every thirty years or so.

Who should be recognized in this project?
Nelson Mandela and Bob Geldof.

What is your favourite food?
Mashed potatoes.

Skinnyman would like to express his thanks to all those who strive to bring about equality for all humankind. Big shout out to www.wateraid.org

Steak Zombies

Steak Zombies is the brainchild of Stoke Newington artist Penelope Grabowski. Penelope creates art, fashion and craft via her workshops, installations, multi-media experiments, exhibitions, characters and patches. Penelope (who paints herself yellow at workshops) and the other artists she collaborates with use the tales and characters from the whimsical Steak Zombies world as a platform for artistic experimentation with graphic characters, plush dolls, stage outfits, theatre costumes and character-based, real-life getups. In a series of live sewing and clothes-customizing performances in clubs and on catwalks, the Steak Zombies play with fashion, highlighting the manufacturing process as a means of artistic expression and entertainment. They have been exhibited at Tate Britain in London and at the Space Downtown gallery in New York.

The story of the Steak Zombies
Once upon a time in an area of the peaceful Zombieland there was a dark and dreadful place with a gigantic factory called 'Sexy Meat Incorporated' that spread towards the horizon. This was a place where it never rained and nothing good ever grew. Except for evil! Hell was under new management, and the new CEO was spinning an evil plan.

In the caves underneath the factory he prepared his strike against all gentle souls of Zombieland. The Devil had made a pact with the factory to give prosperity in exchange for the souls of slaughtered cows. The mean Butcher worked overtime to meet these expectations. But among the herd of cattle for slaughter was Madeleine Bovine, the holy cow.

Soon it was Madeleine's turn. She was daydreaming, watching a butterfly, but then the Butcher grabbed her. As he plunged the knife into her belly, Madeleine farted and in the moment of death and life, a sparkle inflamed a flatulent fart. The Steak Zombie part of her soul emerged in the flame and Madeleine escaped on her own fart. The Devil watched everything and decided to send the Steak Zombie after the cow. But what he didn't know was that the Steak Zombie was not his henchman anymore. He was part of the soul of the holy cow and superhero of the Steak Zombies' saga.

www.steakzombies.com

STEAK ZOMBIES 236

King Adz vs Steak Zombies

When were your formative years?
1994.

Nearest city while growing up?
Stuttgart.

Who, or what, has had an urban influence in the following areas?
MUSIC: *Schneider TM, Cobra Killer, Puppetmastaz, David Bowie, DJ Trinolopez and Björk.*
ART: *Faile, Swoon, London Police, Os Gêmeos, Chaos Computer Club and Pictoplasma.*
DESIGN: *Transmediale and Jonathan Barnbrook.*
ADVERTISING/MEDIA: *Mother, Airside and Wieden+Kennedy.*
FASHION: *Cassette Playa, Tatty Devine, Griffin and Madonna.*
FILM: *Michel Gondry, Rainer Werner Fassbinder, Pedro Almodóvar, 99 Euro Films, Russell Maier, La Haine (Mathieu Kassovitz) and Dogma films (Lars von Trier).*
LITERATURE: *Dostoyevsky, William Gibson and print-on-demand.*
CITY/PLACE: *Berlin, London, New York, São Paulo, Marseille and Buenos Aires.*

How have you made your mark on urban culture?
I impersonate my characters using dolls, workshops and performance, and I involve other artists and the audience in my work too.

What made you realize that urban culture was changing?
Clubs, markets, art happenings outside galleries and street art in galleries.

When was that?
I realized that urban culture was changing when I painted myself yellow and people started to take me more seriously.

Who should be recognized in this project?
Christoph Petersen (with whom I started Steak Zombies) and Dani and Mick (who I collaborate with and who inspire me).

What is your favourite food?
My mum's tortilla de patatas (Spanish omelette) and albondigas (meatballs).

238

STEAK ZOMBIES 2

Chicken bicken

A Brick Lane special. This is a recipe I have been making for fifteen years, and is a typical English 'curry' (it's never been anywhere near India, but it does taste like a rude boy Ruby). Us Brits love a good 'curry'! And this is the one to make if you want to have an 'Indian' night and blow people away.

Feeds 4

1 **onion**
4 **chicken breasts**
a small lump of fresh root ginger, chopped
4 **cloves garlic, chopped**
½ jar **Patak's balti paste (or similar)**
1 bunch **fresh coriander**
6 **curry leaves**
2 teaspoons **each of ground cumin, coriander, turmeric and garam masala**
4 **cardamom pods**
1 **chicken stock cube**
600ml/1 pint/2½ cups **water**
200g/7oz **block of creamed coconut**
1 **green chilli, chopped**
a tablespoon **of butter**

- Chop the onion. However you want. Small is good. Fry until golden. This is important, as you don't want to make everything taste of onion.

- While the onion is cooking, wash and chop the chicken breasts into smallish chunks. Add the chicken to the onion when it looks like it's about to burn. Then add the ginger and the garlic.

- Fry up for 5 minutes or until the chicken turns white. Add the curry paste.

- Chop and add three-quarters of the bunch of coriander (save the rest). Add the curry leaves, ground spices and cardamom pods. Add the stock cube and enough of the water to cover the meat. Put the pan on the lowest heat setting available and cook for 20 minutes.

- Chop the coconut block, then add it to the chicken with the chilli, remaining water and the butter too. Cook for about an hour and then remove from the heat and allow to stand for a couple of hours.

- Gently reheat, sprinkle with the remaining coriander, and serve with basmati rice and/or naan bread.

Jerk chicken with hot pepper gravy

This is a recipe from Ladbroke Grove, West London. A guy I knew back inna day had a shop there selling hip-hop clothes and trainers that he and his partner imported from New York by the bag load (as many as they could get on the plane). This was in 1989 and good gear was hard to get. I used to hang with him sometimes and we'd eat jerk chicken for lunch. Those were the dayz.

Feeds 4

8 chicken portions (thighs and
 drumsticks)
jerk seasoning (Encona or similar)
500g/18oz yoghurt
juice of 1 lime

Hot pepper gravy

2 teaspoons ground allspice
1 teaspoon jerk seasoning
1 chicken stock cube dissolved
 in 450ml/16fl oz/2 cups water
1 tablespoon soy sauce
2 teaspoons chopped garlic
1 teaspoon chopped fresh root ginger

- Wash the chicken pieces and score each piece deeply with a sharp knife three or four times.

- In a large bowl mix 1–4 teaspoons of jerk seasoning (depending on how hot you want it!) with the yoghurt and lime juice, and then add all the chicken pieces, one by one, coating each piece with the mixture. Marinate for as long as possible (overnight is best).

- Bake in the oven at 200°C/400°F/Gas 6 for 60 minutes, or else cook on a BBQ for 30 minutes.

- Meanwhile, make the hot pepper gravy. Mix all the ingredients in a pan and bring to the boil.

- Simmer for 10 minutes.

- Serve the jerk chicken with rice and peas and hot pepper gravy.

Rice and Peas

I used to live in Balham, South London, and my flatmate's mum would send round rice and peas and hot pepper gravy on a Sunday (a Jamaican Sunday lunch). This was the best thing we'd eat all week.

Feeds 4–6

300g/11oz long-grain rice
1 bunch spring onions (or just a regular onion), chopped
1 can kidney beans
4 teaspoons allspice
4 tablespoons soy sauce
4 cloves garlic, chopped (or 4 teaspoons garlic paste from a jar)
1 chicken stock cube
200g/7oz block of creamed coconut

- Wash the rice and cover with water to about 3cm/1in above the top of the rice. Mix the onion into the rice and water. Open the can of kidney beans and pour into the rice, brine and all. Add the allspice, soy sauce, garlic and stock cube. Chop the coconut block into pieces and add to the mixture.

- Mix thoroughly and then cover the pan and bring to the boil. Cook for 20 minutes on a very low heat without taking off the lid.

- Turn off the heat and allow the pan to stand for 10 minutes before serving with jerk chicken and hot pepper gravy (see the recipe above).

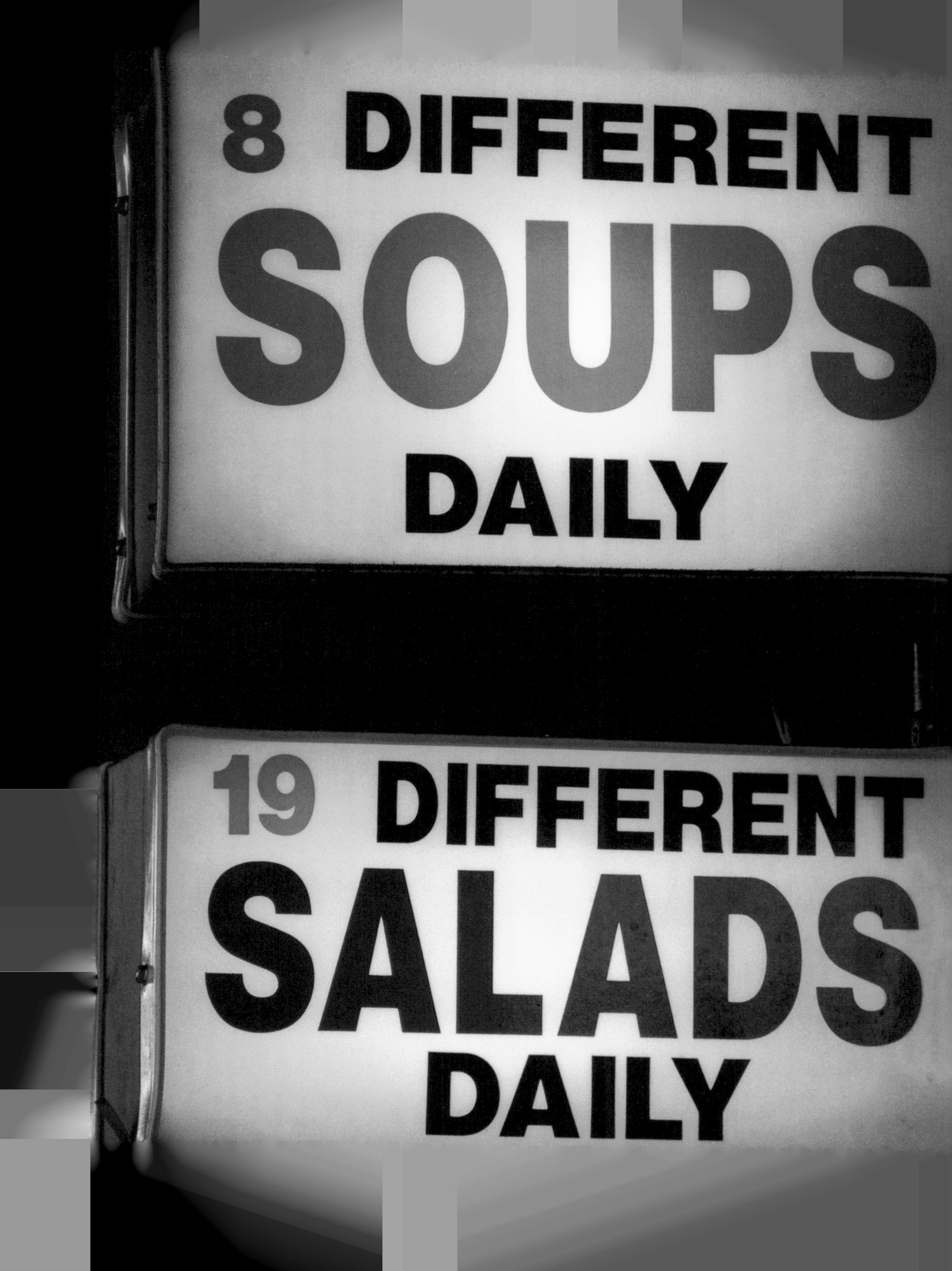
8 DIFFERENT
SOUPS
DAILY
19 DIFFERENT
SALADS
DAILY

TWO SOUPS

Easy does it. These are the easiest soups to make and they taste like nothing else. You (and your friends) will be amazed at your skills in the kitchen. You'd get both in London: one in an old-school bistro and the other in Chinatown.

Asparagus and chilli soup

Feeds 2
1 **large bunch asparagus**
350ml/12floz/1½ cups **water**
1 **chicken stock cube**
1 **small red chilli or a dash of chilli oil**
150ml/5fl oz **cream**
ground black pepper

- Chop the asparagus into small pieces and boil in a medium pan with the water.

- When the water is boiling, add the stock cube and simmer until the asparagus is cooked, about 10 minutes maximum.

- Add the chilli or chilli oil (how hot is up to you) and blend with a hand blender. Once blended, add the cream, season with pepper, stir and remove the pan from the heat.

- Serve with crispy rolls and salted butter.

Fish ball soup

Feeds 4–6

2 **chicken stock cubes**
900ml/1½ pints/4¼ cups **water**
10 thin slices **fresh root ginger, as much
  or as little as you like**
300g/11oz **plain or chilli-flavoured fried
  fish balls**
300g/11oz **fried fish roll, sliced (you can
  get both of the above ingredients from
  a Chinese supermarket)**
85g/3oz **watercress**
salt and black pepper

• Dissolve the stock cubes in the water in a large pan, and then add the sliced ginger.

• Bring to the boil. Add the fish balls and the sliced fish meat roll, and heat through.

• Wash and tear apart the watercress then add to the pan. Add salt and pepper. Done. Couldn't be simpler. Chinatown here you come…

Spaghetti pie

A new twist to the old classic. This is an English variation of an Americanised Italian recipe that makes a 'pie' out of something (although there is no pastry).

Feeds 8

1 **large onion, chopped**
1kg/2¼lb **minced ground beef
(steak is best)**
1 large can **tomatoes (or use passata
if you're posh)**
4 tablespoons **tomato purée**
2 **beef stock cubes dissolved in**
100ml/3½fl oz/nearly ½ cup **water**
4 **cloves garlic, chopped**
a splash **of red wine**
4 teaspoons **Italian dried herbs**
plenty of salt and black pepper
a handful of **fresh basil, chopped**
about 600g/1lb 5oz **spaghetti**
25g/1oz **butter**
2 heaped dessert spoons **cornflour**
425ml/¾ pint/scant 2 cups **milk**
400g/14oz **Cheddar cheese, grated**
2 teaspoons **mustard**
8 slices **Emmental cheese**
a large bunch of **fresh spinach**

- Fry the chopped onion until cooked. Add the meat, and cook on a low heat until the colour of the meat darkens. Add the tomatoes (can and purée), stock, garlic, wine and herbs, and enough water to cover. Bring to the boil and then simmer for about 2 hours, stirring and adding water every 20 minutes – keep it moist!

- After the meat sauce has been cooking for at least 1½ hours, boil a large pan of water and under-cook the spaghetti for 6–8 minutes.

- In another pan, melt the butter, add the cornflour and mix into a stiff paste. Add the milk splash by splash, mixing the paste constantly to avoid lumps, and then return to the heat. Add three-quarters of the grated Cheddar and all the mustard to the milk/cornflour mixture and heat, stirring continually. The cheese will melt and the sauce will thicken. Once thickened, stir for 5 minutes and then turn off the heat.

- In a colander, pour boiling water over the spinach to part cook it.

- In a large ovenproof dish, place a layer of spaghetti, then a layer of meat sauce, then 4 slices of Emmental cheese, then a layer of spinach, then a layer of cheese sauce … repeat twice. Sprinkle the remaining grated Cheddar on top and bake in the oven at 190°C/375°F/Gas 5 until the cheese is golden brown, about 25 minutes.

Fisherman's pie

Shiver me timbers! This is straight out of an old East End caff, before it was refurbished, and is probably the most traditional English street food recipe in this book. It's very easy to make and really healthy to boot!

Feeds 4
450g/1lb **potatoes**
700g/1½lb **white fish (haddock or cod)**
a tablespoon **of butter**
400ml/14fl oz/1¾ cups **milk**
2 heaped tablespoons cornflour
a handful of **fresh parsley, chopped**
salt and black pepper
2 teaspoons **cream (optional)**
100g/4oz **Cheddar cheese, grated**

- Peel and boil the potatoes until cooked.

- Cook the fish in a frying pan with a smidge of the butter and a splash of milk for about 10 minutes.

- In another pan, melt half of the butter and add the cornflour. Add the milk and parsley and stir continually until thickened.

- Mash the potatoes with the remaining butter and add a dash of milk or the cream. Season to taste.

- Place the cooked fish in the bottom of an ovenproof dish and cover with mash. Sprinkle the grated cheese on top and bake in the oven at 190°C/375°F/Gas 5 until golden brown, about 20 minutes.

FRESH FISH

ইবকো ব্রান্ড বাংলাদেশী তাজা মাছ

Prawn

Green Thai curry

Big props to all the Thais who have braved the shitty English weather and have made sure that we can get hold of a decent bit of Thai cooking in the UK. I'm a big big fan of really hot Thai food, but this is a cool (temperature-wise) English version of a Thai classic.

Feeds 4–6

2 tablespoons cooking oil
1 **onion, chopped**
3 tablespoons **green Thai curry paste**
1 tablespoon **soft dark brown sugar**
1 stalk **lemongrass, chopped**
3 teaspoons **each of garlic and ginger pastes**
4 **chicken breasts, chopped into** 2cm/¾in cubes **(use tofu instead for a veggie option)**
400ml/14oz **coconut milk**
2 tablespoons **soy sauce, or to taste**
500g/18oz **new potatoes**
250g/9oz **green beans, halved**
lots of **fresh coriander, chopped**
juice of 2 **limes**
250g/9oz **mushrooms, halved**

- Heat the oil in a wok or a large frying pan, and fry the onion until golden. Add the green curry paste and sugar and cook on a high heat for about a minute, before stirring in the lemongrass and garlic and ginger pastes. Add the chicken pieces and make sure they are fully coated in the paste.

- Add the coconut milk and soy sauce and heat gently, simmering for 25–30 minutes, until the sauce has thickened slightly.

- Meanwhile, boil the potatoes in a separate pan.

- Stir the green beans, coriander, lime juice and mushrooms into the curry paste mixture. Then add the boiled potatoes too, and simmer for a further 10 minutes.

- Serve with basmati rice or Thai noodles.

10 more things...

10 Books

Martin Amis, *Time's Arrow, or, The Nature of the Offence* (1991)

Paul Bowles, *The Sheltering Sky* (1949)

E. L. Doctorow, *Ragtime* (1975)

Tama Janowitz, *Slaves of New York* (1986)

Rohinton Mistry, *A Fine Balance* (1995)

R. K. Narayan, *Malgudi Days* (1982)

Ben Okri, Stars of the New Curfew (1988)

Hergé (Georges Prosper Rémi), *The Adventures of Tintin* (1929–83)

Michel van Rijn, *Hot Art, Cold Cash* (1993)

Faldela Williams, *The Cape Malay Illustrated Cookbook* (1998)

10 Films

Woody Allen, *Manhattan* (1979)

Ingmar Bergman, *Persona* (1966)

Nick Broomfield, *The Leader, His Driver and the Driver's Wife* (1991)

Mike Clattenburg, *Trailer Park Boys: The Movie* (2006)

Federico Fellini, *8½* (1963)

Werner Herzog, *The White Diamond* (2004)

Tony Kaye, *American History X* (1998)

Krzysztof Kieslowski, *The Decalogue* (1989)

Stacy Peralta, *Dogtown and Z-Boys* (2001)

Lars von Trier, *Dancer in the Dark* (2000)

10 Albums

Maria Callas, *The Golden Voice of Maria Callas* (1995)

DJ Cam, *Substances* (1996)

Kruder & Dorfmeister, *The K & D Sessions* (1998)

Lee 'Scratch' Perry (with Dub Syndicate), *Time Boom X – De Devil Dead* (1987)

Sigur Rós, *Takk* (2005)

Scientist, *Scientist Meets the Space Invaders* (1981)

Skinnyman, *Council Estate of Mind* (2004)

David Sylvian, *Gone to Earth* (ambient side) (1986)

TBR (Tom Robinson Band), *Power in the Darkness* (1978)

Underworld, *Oblivion with Bells* (2007)

10 Websites

www.**100proof**.tv

www.**adhunt.blogspot**.com

www.**burningflags**.com

www.**kolahstudio**.com

www.**michelvanrijn**.nl

www.**plastickid**.dk

www.**shift**.jp.org

www.**supertouchblog**.com

www.**wmmna**.com

www.**xplicid**.com

Acknowledgments

In loving memory of Matt Webster – 1 September 1979 to 17 September 2003

Biggest props to: Wilma, Kaiya and Casius for always being down with me despite my madness; Mum and Beardy for letting me run loose and wild when I was a youth; Jayne, Dave, Andy and Jono (the bear that fell out of a tree) for backing me up no matter what; Conrad and Michelle for teaching me how to really cook; Alex and Thandiwe Mamacos (big up Cape Town); my O. G. Homeboy Irvin & Hannah; Walksy and Kirsten; Sean, Mia and Lois; Matt Hampshire; Lee 'Slippy' O'Neill; Heavy Lee; Daniel and Lawrence Eccleston; John and Heather Roderick (big up India); Rasjad (Barrie) and Latimah; Ellie; Jonathan Olley (Bruv!); Sophie and Oscar (Quack!); Marina and Dan; Liza and Matt; and last but definitely not least, Pete Case for being there for me when it really mattered (you know the score).

Big Love for all 100proof soldiers and those who have got down with my click over the years: Jamie Camplin and Sam Clark at Thames & Hudson, Paul Sellars, John Pace, DJ Cam, Lenny Let Loose Lennox, Robin Dean, D*Face, Beka Cohen, Tristan Eaton, Skinnyman, Hendrix, Laser 3.14, A1one Writer from Iran, Sputn*kk, Brad Downey, Paul Hartnett, Craig Fairbrass, Dr Revolt, Dize, Nina Köll, Erik Kessels and Sabine Gilhuijs, Miss Blackbirdy, Helmut Smits, Rodney Smith, Adam Schatz, Jon Setzen, Boogie, Steve and Rilla at Rinzen, Penelope 'Steak Zombies' Grabowski, Invader, JR, Elisabeth Arkhipoff, Marc and Sara Schiller, Leti and Pleix, eBoy, Martin Eberle, Juan Vandervoort and Horst Weidenmüller, Anne-Faye Townsend and Darrell Berry, Dr. D, Maya Deren, Faith 47, Nathan Reddy, J. P. Roussouw, Mike Shallit, Nick Wittenberg, Sir Cliff Richard, Q'am from Batley and Brad from Morley, Charlotte Ellis and Kent Baker and DJ Ready D.

Inspiration for everything I've ever done has flowed through the work of these people: E. L. Doctorow, Werner Herzog, DJ Cam, David Sylvian, Lee 'Scratch' Perry, Martin Amis, Andy Warhol, Colin Hay, Maria Callas, Nas, Tama Janowitz, Hergé and his boy Tintin, all youths running wild, waxing and milking it for all their worth, all skaters, all the outcasts, the bergies and the skollies, DJ Shadow, the Beastie Boys, KLF, Dog Town and the Z-Boys/Stacy Peralta, Scientist (Everton Brown), Henry 'Junjo' Lawes, Bret Easton Ellis and R. K. Narayan.

Just so you know:
King Tubby/Vidor/Ad Rock (KING) + Advertising/Adam (ADZ) = KING ADZ

Picture Credits

All photographs by King Adz unless otherwise specified. p. 1, foreground, rat stencil by Banksy; pp. 2–3, film still by Pleix (www.pleix.net); pp. 12–13, artwork and designs by Elisabeth Arkhipoff, D*Face, Brad Downey, 'G', Kessels Kramer, Miss Blackbirdy, Jonathan Olley, Pleix (www.pleix.net), Rinzen, Helmut Smits, Steak Zombies; pp. 14–15, left to right, from top: photo of Rodney Smith by Allen Ying, photo of woman by Boogie, drawing by Jon Setzen, toy designs by Tristan Eaton, street art by WK Interact; pp. 22–23, photo of Wooster on Spring project by Michael Simon, artwork and designs by Bast, Bozack Nation, D*Face, Faile, JR, Neckface, Obey, Stay High 149, Judith Supine; pp. 24, 26–27, photos by Boogie; p. 28, photo of Tristan Eaton by Matthias Clamer, illustration by Tristan Eaton; pp. 29–33, toy designs by Tristan Eaton; p. 34, Things I Love About New York by Jon Setzen; pp. 36–37, collages by Jon Setzen; p. 38, photo by Bill Thomas; p. 41, photo by Allen Ying; p. 43, photo by Shut; pp. 44–47, artwork by Above, Blek Le Rat, Bloo, D*Face, London Police, Thundercut, all photos by Michael Simon; pp. 62–63, artwork by Invader, l'Atlas, Obey; pp. 70–71, artwork by Brode, c215, Dr Revolt, Gonzo, Invader, Mimi the Clown, Miss Tic, Pimix, Pure Evil, Sun7, Judith Supine; pp. 72–73, artwork by Elisabeth Arkhipoff; p. 75, artwork by Elisabeth Arkhipoff and Laurent Fétis; pp. 82–85, all photos by JR; pp. 86–87, 89, 91, film stills by Pleix (www.pleix.net); pp. 92–95, all artwork by Invader; pp. 110–11, artwork and designs by London Police, Rinzen; pp. 118–19; artwork by Alias, Dolk, Brad Downey, M-City, Swoon; pp. 120–21, 123, photos by Martin Eberle; p. 124, artwork by eBoy; p. 125, shoe design by eBoy for DKNY; pp. 126–27, artwork by eBoy; p. 129, photos by Jason Evans; p. 133, design by www.nonformat.com; pp. 134–35, designs by Rinzen; pp. 136–37, artwork by Lyn Balzer, Tony Perkins and Rinzen, photo by Balzer and Perkins; p. 139, design by Rinzen; p. 140, photo by King Adz of a Martha Cooper photo; pp. 158–59, artwork and designs by Hendrix, Kessels Kramer, London Police, Mir, Popof, Recalone, Wolf & Pack; pp. 166–67, artwork and designs by Amer, Fafi, Justin Kees, Kessels Kramer, Laser 3.14, London Police, Recalone; pp. 168, 173, photos by Ivo Hofste; pp. 174–76, 178–79, designs by Kessels Kramer; p. 182, photo by Nina Köll, photo collage by King Adz; pp. 188–191, artwork and photos by Helmut Smits; pp. 206–07, photos, left to right: D*Face, Penelope Grabowski, Jonathan Olley, artwork and designs by D*Face, Jonathan Olley, Steak Zombies; pp. 214–15, artwork by Banksy, D*Face, Eine, Faile, Pure Evil, Judith Supine, Asbstos, all Polaroid photos by Paul Hartnett; p. 217, photo by Darrell Berry; p. 221, sculpture and photo by D*Face; p. 222, artwork and photo by D*Face; p. 225, installation and photo by D*Face; pp. 226, 228–30, photos by Jonathan Olley; pp. 236–39, all artwork by Steak Zombies, photos by Penelope Grabowski